DOUGLAS A RYAN

BUSINESS ASPECTS OF CATERING

Longman Scientific & Technical,
Longman Group UK Limited,
Longman House, Burnt Mill, Harlow,
Essex CM20 2JE, England
and Associated Companies throughout the world.

Published in the United States of America
by Longman Inc., New York

First published 1989

British Library Cataloguing in Publication Data

Ryan, Douglas A.
    Business aspects of catering.
    1. Great Britain. Catering industries
    I. Title
    647'.95'068

ISBN 0-582-01852-8

Produced by Longman Group (FE) Limited
Printed in Hong Kong

CONTENTS

PREFACE

This book has been written at an introductory level for those in catering who are either preparing for external examinations or who wish to learn about the business aspects of catering at a practical but simple level. The text covers the requirements of various syllabuses, but in particular the syllabuses for City & Guilds 706 and 707. It will be of immense value for those studying for City & Guilds 717, National Examination Board for Supervisory Studies Supervisory Course (Catering) and as an introduction to the Business and Supervisory Studies Unit of Hotel, Catering and Institutional Management, Part I. The book will also be a very useful additional source of information and assistance for a number of units of the Business and Technical Education Council First Diploma and Certificate in Hotel and Catering Studies, and National Diploma and Certificate in Hotel, Catering and Institutional Operations.

With catering assuming greater importance in the country's economy a significant input of financial and legal matters is being introduced to all courses. The book contains sufficient information for the requirements of these courses and at the same time provides an outline for further study. At a practical level the book provides guidelines for small operators who may be seeking new ideas or who may wish to update their knowledge of business techniques.

There is a variety of business-studies texts available for catering and these fall into two general categories. In the first group are those which must be used with the assistance of a teacher or necessitating reference to other books. In the other group lie those which are too simple for any serious study or which offer no practical application. *Business Aspects of Catering* sets out to cover the gap left by these two groups. It is written in simple language, in an easily understood manner but offering discriminatory material related to the industry.

The text is divided into three Parts. Part I gives an introduction to the hotel and catering industry and also deals with the routines of purchasing and supply. It takes the reader through the process of control starting with purchasing and ordering then to receiving, storing and issuing. The financial and costs aspects are considered in Part II. This covers dish costing, gross and net profit, forecasting and selling, yields and wastage and elements of costs and budgeting. Part III concentrates on various aspects of catering law in a clear, systematic way. This relieves the reader from having to refer to numerous law books to learn about licensing, employment law, hygiene and health and safety legislation. The condensing and simplification of a complex subject such as this should be a welcome feature in a book of this sort.

Part IV contains the appendices which include a self-assessment test in catering calculations together with explanations and practice in conversions, percentages and temperatures. This has been included to assist those who need to revise basic catering calculations. An important aspect of this book is the number of calculations included simulating real situations. It is hoped that this will give the user practice and confidence.

At the end of each chapter there is a summary listing the main points. This summary, together with the self-assessment questions which are provided, assists the reader in understanding the contents.

The hotel and catering industry rates as the second-largest industry for bankruptcies. Many of these are a result of the owner's lack of business understanding. For this purpose a chapter (Ch. 16) has been included setting out many points of useful information aimed at helping the reader with planning. While the chapter does not profess to teach how to run a business it does provide valuable information for those contemplating setting up in business.

Thanks are due to my wife, Paulette, for her encouragement and assistance with typing, to Glen Mealing of Westminster College for his valuable comments and to John Brawn of Garnett College for his advice and editorial assistance.

Throughout the book we have used the pronoun 'he' when referring to people. The usage has been for convenience and in no way do we ignore the important role of women in this industry.

ACKNOWLEDGEMENTS

We are indebted to the following for permission to reproduce copyright material:

British Tourist Authority for our Fig. 1.1; Dukes Hotel for our Exhibit 12.1; Fitch & Son Ltd. for our Exhibits 3.5–3.6; Grosvenor Hotel for our Exhibit 3.2; Hotel & Catering Training Board for our Figs. 1.2–1.8; Kalamazoo PLC for our Exhibit 4.2; Royal Garden Hotel for our Exhibit 4.3; Twinlock Ltd. for our Exhibit 4.1 and Unifood for Table 2.3

We are indebted to the following for permission to reproduce copyright material:

...

INTRODUCTION

Whether one is considering a hotel, a restaurant, a hospital kitchen or a college canteen, all share the same aim of providing a service in the form of accommodation or food and drink away from home. A commercial enterprise seeks to make a profit by buying, processing and selling food and drinks or providing accommodation. An institutional organisation, e.g. a hospital kitchen, while it may not have the profit motive as its main objective, nevertheless must run the operation within certain financial constraints imposed by the Government or the particular authority responsible. Similarly, a non-profit-making organisation, e.g. a private badminton club, which has the provision of services and facilities to members as its main objective may, however, seek to have a surplus, that is, an excess of income over expenditure. In all instances, the operation must be run efficiently and effectively to attain its aim of providing a service and at the same time either making a profit or keeping within the required financial limits.

In order to achieve this it is necessary to exercise strict control. Many factors concerned with planning and organisation need to be balanced. These factors are associated with how costs and sales of food and drinks are to be controlled. Food and beverage control can be defined as 'a management process concerned with planning, regulating and directing all food and drink costs and activities related to those costs'. Food and beverage control is a continuous process from the time the food or drinks are ordered until they are sold to, or provided for, the customer. It involves purchasing, receiving, storage and issuing, preparation and cooking, and finally serving and selling.

Throughout this process people are involved in handling large amounts of money, both in the form of cash and goods, and therefore food and beverage control must include the control and direction of staff. The wrong-sized bag does not appear by accident in the kitchen. It has either been ordered wrongly or wrongly delivered and carelessly received. Food spoilage arises from incorrect storage or because excessive quantities are issued from stores and are not used. A joint of meat does not suddenly shrink by itself. Again it has either been wrongly bought, badly prepared or badly cooked. Food does not walk out of the kitchen. Any shortage happens because items have not been charged to the customer in the restaurant or bar, or have been wasted through serving oversized portions or through spillages, or have been stolen or consumed by staff. All along the line loss can occur through wastage or spoilage for which people are responsible.

Management is ultimately responsible for any food and beverage operation, and control is the means by which this responsibility is executed. There are various means of control available to management. These may differ from one establishment to another and what may be suitable for one is not necessarily suitable for another. There are, however, certain principles of control which are applicable to all, and control systems are discussed throughout. These include establishing standards of quality and quantity; setting up procedures to be adopted for specific activities; keeping accurate and regular records; preparing financial records with details of transactions; and preparing budgets. These principles are adaptable to suit individual and particular circumstances. For example, a large luxury hotel with numerous personnel handling large amounts of expensive items will require a more elaborate system of control than a small 'husband-and-wife operation' by the seaside.

The hotel and catering industry has inherited many traditional systems which, because of the availability of cheap labour, were possible at the time. The increased cost of labour has forced many to minimise staff numbers and streamline paperwork. Much of the work is now being done by computers which take the strain off management. Computers can perform any routine or repetitive function in a shorter time, more accurately and efficiently than by manual methods.

GLOSSARY

Accounting: Term used for recording all financial transactions of a business and using the information to assist management in making decisions.

Accounting period: A period of time suitable to the particular operation during which time the financial position of the establishment may be determined.

Acquisition: The buying out of smaller businesses by other larger organisations.

Bankruptcy: A business which cannot continue operating because of its inability to pay its debts goes into bankruptcy.

Beverages: A beverage is simply a drink. In the catering industry beverages are classified between alcoholic and non-alcoholic.

Blind receiving: Receiving goods for which amounts and weights are unknown to the receiving clerk. This ensures more care and accuracy in checking.

Brand: Usually an established product generally recognised by name.

Bulk buying: Buying in large quantities so as to obtain goods at a cheaper price.

Capital: There are a number of different interpretations of capital, but its more common meaning is as the money necessary to start a business.

Cash: This is money in the form of banknotes and coins.

Cash flow: The difference between cash (including cheques) coming into the business and that going out of the business at a particular period of time. It must not be confused with profit.

Centralisation: Concentration of all financial activities of various outlets into one centre.

Central buying: Suitable for large organisations, in practice it means that apart from local purchases of very small value, all purchases are made from a central office which 'resells' to the units within the organisation.

Code of practice: Official advice but not having the force of law.

Consortium: The voluntary grouping of small businesses governed by self-imposed rules. It gives the members of the consortium more buying power and better shared marketing and sales strategies. All members keep their own individual identity and control.

Contract buying: Buying a particular range of commodities from a supplier for a fixed amount during a fixed period at a fixed price.

Contract caterers: Operators specialising in the provision of canteen facilities to workers.

Convenience food: Food sold by manufacturers in a state of preparation requiring the minimum amount of processing before serving.

Convenience stores: A shop which combines the old-fashioned corner shop with modern fast-food technology.

Cook–chill: A system of producing meals by conventional methods then chilling rapidly and storing at 3 °C for up to 6 days.

Depreciation: All assets have a limited useful life. The reduction in value is charged as an expense of the business. This charge is the depreciation.

Dish-costing card: A form used for costing standard recipes.

Dry stores: Food stores for non-perishable goods.

Fast food: A sector of the industry concerned with preparing speedily and selling food and drink for consumption on or off the premises.

Food cost: The cost of materials, i.e. food and drink, prepared for sale.

Forecasting: Anticipating the volume of sales.

Franchise: A system in which a company allows another company or individual to sell its products for an agreed fee.

Franchisee: The company or individual using the franchise and paying the fee.

Franchisor: The company granting the franchise.

Freehold: When the business owns the premises from which it operates, the premises are referred to as freehold.

Industry: A group of firms or organisations involved in the production of a particular type of goods or services.

Leasehold: Not all businesses own the building from where they carry out their activities. They therefore contract with the owners of the building to use it by paying a rent. The contract is known as a lease.

Material cost: See food cost.

Multinationals: Large organisations with subsidiaries spread throughout the world.

National Insurance: A form of tax used by Government to pay unemployment benefits, sickness benefits and state pensions. Part of this tax is paid by the employee and part by the employer.

Operational staff: Workers at craft level and below performing the manual work necessary to run the business.

Popular catering: Preparation and selling of specialised food of a particular quality.

Portion control: A system of checking that the actual portions achieved correspond to those estimated.

Purchases: Goods bought for resale.

Recipe card: A form used for recording recipes accurately.

Requisition: Request for supplies from stores.

Requisition form: A document used to authorise requests for issues from stores.

Salaries: Remuneration paid to staff on a monthly basis.

Security: The protection of buildings, stock, equipment and customers' property from loss or damage.

Service charge: A charge made to the customer to cover the cost of labour.

Standardisation: The conforming by all outlets in a particular operation to set standards, colours, design, service, menu.

Staff turnover: The number of staff leaving or replaced.

Standard recipe: A recipe for food or beverage of a specified quality and quantity for use in a particular establishment.

Stock: Food and beverage items available for resale at the establishment.

Stocktaking: Valuing, in money terms, the stock at the end of a period.

Tribunal: A court of law which limits its business to matters relating to specific areas, e.g. industrial tribunal.

Tronc: A collection of tips to be divided out later.

Ullage: Loss of beverage through natural causes, e.g. imperfect wines, sediment, unavoidable waste.

VAT: Value added tax. A tax on all sales and services.

Vending: A merchandising machine which dispenses a variety of food products for immediate consumption.

Wages: Remuneration paid to workers on a weekly basis.

Yield: The final amount of portions of food or drink obtainable.

PART I

PART 1.

1

INTRODUCTION TO THE HOTEL AND CATERING INDUSTRY

As we look into this industry it is important to remember that people have a basic need for accommodation, food and drink. While this is normally provided in the home there are many instances when it has to be provided away from home. The hotel and catering industry provides for this need through a variety of undertakings from prisons to luxury hotels or from college canteens to top-class restaurants. Operations in the hotel and catering industry can be roughly divided under the headings shown in Table 1.1.

Before studying this industry we may find it useful to take a brief look at its history. Hospitality activities have existed from time immemorial. Perhaps the best reference to this is the story of Christmas when Mary and Joseph unsuccessfully sought shelter in an inn.

During the Roman occupation of Britain when the first roads were built, merchants and other wealthy travellers journeyed to various parts of the country. At points on their journeys, shelter, food and drink were to be found at roadside taverns. Later on, the monasteries provided hospitality to raise money for the Church. The monasteries offered adequate services which were to continue over a long period until political events saw their dissolution.

The need for these services continued and they were later to be provided by the large manor-houses scattered throughout the country. Economic development brought changes in the life of the country and manor-houses began to be taxed. In order to raise money to meet these taxes the lords of the manors began converting their homes into inns. It is interesting to note that as far back as 1550 laws existed concerning accommodation premises. An inn could provide rest but a tavern could provide only food and drink. The inns and taverns remained for a long time and gradually their provision of rest, food and drink improved in quality and standard.

The nineteenth century saw a number of innovations which greatly affected the hotel and catering industry. The earlier part of

TABLE 1.1 Operations in the Hotel and Catering Industry.

Public services	Pubs/Clubs	Hotels
Armed forces	Banqueting halls	Bed and breakfast
Children's homes	Bars	Boarding house
Colleges	Bingo halls	Boarding school
Convalescent homes	Casinos	Camping sites
Halls of residence	Clubs	Caravan sites
Hospices	Dance-halls	Conference centres
Hospitals	Discothèques	Guest houses
Local authorities	Leisure centres	Holiday camps
Meals-on-wheels	Night-clubs	Holiday flats
Nursing homes	Pub food counters	Hostels
Old people's homes	Pubs	Hotels
Parks	Sports clubs	Merchant ships
Prisons	Wine bars	Motels
School meals	Working men's clubs	Private hospitals
		Residential homes
		Staff homes

the century saw development of the railway system begin. More and more travellers changed from road to rail which brought a decline in the use of inns and taverns. Many of them vanished, but others became the forerunners of many of our pubs today. The railway companies met the demands from passengers by building hotels at, or near, the railway termini. Easier travel and more spending money as a result of industrial development saw the expansion of holiday resorts. Steamships brought continents closer together and provided their wealthy customers with luxurious accommodation at sea. On land these wealthy passengers demanded appropriate hotel accommodation. In response hotels such as the Savoy and Claridges were built followed by a long string of other luxury hotels.

The last 50 years has witnessed many changes and innovations in the industry. The revolution in air travel has meant jets transporting millions of people across the world annually. Motorway travel has had its implication for the industry with a demand for accommodation and food on or near the motorways. An ever-increasing movement of goods and people to and from Europe has created a demand for ferry services.

Catering services	Restaurants	Contract/Industrial
Aircraft	Bistros	Canteens
Art galleries	Burger bars	Contract caterers
Cinemas	Cafés	Factory canteens
Exhibition halls	Cafeterias	Office canteens
Ferries	Chinese etc. take-away	Oil rigs
In-stores	Doughnut bars	
Liners	Fast-food outlets	
Motorway services	Fish and chip shops	
Museums	Hot-dog stalls	
Race meetings	Ice-cream parlours	
Sporting events	Kebab houses	
Sports centres	Milk bars	
Stately homes	Pancake house	
Theatres	Pizzerias	
Tourist centres	Restaurants	
Trains	Snack-bars	
Travel terminals	Steak-house	
Zoos	Take aways	
	Tea-rooms	

More free time and more ways to spend it, together with higher real incomes has brought an increased demand for leisure pastimes of which 'eating out' is one of the more popular pursuits.

The hotel and catering industry is often thought of as simply dealing with hotels and restaurants, when in fact these are only one group of a much larger family. An industry is a group of firms or organisations involved in the production of goods or services of a particular type. Therefore, as we mentioned earlier, the hotel and catering industry covers commercial as well as non-commercial establishments where food, drink and accommodation of some form or another is provided (Table 1.1). Each establishment will have its particular type of customer; for example, a seaside hotel will tend to specialise in activities suitable for holidaymakers. Other hotels will concentrate on business people and will therefore have conference facilities with secretarial services. A council home is set up to look after children in need of care, or old people or handicapped persons. A prison will need to provide food and bedding for prisoners. A snack-bar will provide a quick light meal, while a quality restaurant will provide a more elaborate meal with waiter service. Every establishment will provide for the comfort of

TABLE 1.2 Types of customers

Public services	Pubs/clubs	Hotels
SP Children in need	SPS Dancers	TS Businessmen
SS Homeless	SPS Drinkers	SS Campers
SP Incurably ill	PS Gamblers	TS Delegates
SS Nurses	TS Members	TS Holidaymakers
SP Patients	Revellers	TS Lodgers
SS Prisoners	SPS Sportsmen	SP Patients
S Schoolchildren		SPS Sales reps
SS Service personnel		SS Seamen
SS Students		SP Tourists
		TS Travellers

its customers. The customer can be a prisoner, sick person, wealthy diner, traveller, etc. Different types of customers can be classified roughly under the same headings (see Table 1.2). However, the major activity will be the same, that is, the provision of food and drink and accommodation.

The industry has seen many changes and innovations in the last 20 years. One of the most important has been the acquisition of companies by other companies and the expansion of these throughout the commercial sector of the industry. This has meant not only the accumulation of wealth but also the development of a more sophisticated system of management and supervision. Most of the activities, such as marketing, purchasing, accounting have been centralised, i.e. the concentration of all the activities in one centre. Competition has increased and with it the standard of service.

Naturally, smaller operations have suffered from this powerful competition, but it has made them more innovative. Many of them have acquired a reputation for their own speciality or peculiarity. Some have grouped together, to form a consortium, to improve their purchasing and marketing capabilities. Standardisation is a necessary requirement for the larger organisations and this has made the smaller operators devote themselves to the needs of those customers who seek individuality and non-conformity.

A growing sector of the industry is that devoted to fast food or popular catering. This is concerned with preparing and serving food to the customer very quickly. There are different levels of operation from the quick 'take-away' service through to a steakhouse. However, they all have very similar characteristics. The menu is usually limited and geared to a specialisation, e.g.

Catering services	Restaurants	Contract/Industrial
Lorry drivers	Diners	Factory workers
Motorists	Families	Office personnel
Shoppers	~~Travellers~~	Wedding guests
Visitors		
~~Wedding guests~~		

hamburgers or pizzas. Most of the food is pre-portioned and there is very little preparation. With outlets owned by large chains, the standardisation is obvious. The outlets' opening times are very flexible, opening almost all day. This places a heavy reliance on a large volume of passing trade and therefore siting is very important. As food is eaten on or off the premises, fewer staff are required. The larger organisations rely considerably on their marketing with extensive use of their logo, very bright colours and imaginative give-aways all playing their part.

Many of these fast-food enterprises are franchises. Franchising is discussed in more detail in Chapter 16 but, very briefly described, it is a form of business mostly suitable for the commercially inexperienced who want to set up on their own. In return for an agreed fee the owners of a franchise will allow the businessman to use their name and sell their products. They will also assist in setting up the operation and will provide training and assist with marketing.

In general, franchises are associated with hamburgers and pizzas, but in the hotel and catering industry, luxury hotel groups like Sheraton, Holiday Inn and Hilton operate a franchise system. However, in the British High Street one can see names like, 'Strikes', 'Spud-U-Like', 'Pizza Express', 'Pizza Hut' and 'Burger King' to mention but a few. Wimpy and Kentucky were the first in the UK. McDonald's, while a major franchise operation in the USA, only granted its first two franchises in the UK in 1986. All other McDonalds in the UK are owned and run by themselves.

The provision of canteen facilities to employees (industrial catering) goes back a long time. In modern business the provision of canteens is an important fringe benefit to employees. This service is either free to employees or highly subsidised by the employer. Many firms organise their own operation, others engage a firm of contract caterers to provide the service.

The old-style factory canteens serving heavily laden plates with unattractive and indifferently prepared food is fast disappearing. The style and speed of service, menu content, food presentation and restuarant atmosphere is designed to attract the workforce, and therefore a professional and more increasingly commercial approach is necessary. Many firms prefer to pass on this responsibility to the experts in this field and therefore contract caterers are appointed. The firm will pay the caterers a fee for feeding its employees. The contract is normally awarded for a period of between 1 and 5 years. Contract caterers cope with all types of industrial catering from the provision of a cafeteria service in a small firm to a variety of facilities in a multinational organisation.

Tourism is a very important sector of the industry. It is a source of income and a creator of employment. The Government, appreciating the value of tourism to the economy seeks to attract foreign tourists by promoting the UK abroad.

British people are taking more holidays than ever before, both abroad and at home. The traditional 2 weeks' holiday by the seaside is being replaced by a new pattern of short breaks. Hence the increased amount of advertising being done by many hotels offering bargain weekends. Caravans and camping holidays are also popular, and together with holiday camps produced an income in 1984 of £420 m. There are a number of firms which specialise in holiday camps among which are Butlins, Pontins, Warners, Ladbroke Holidays and Haven Leisures.

According to the British Tourist Authority (BTA), Britain earned £6,676 m. in foreign currency from tourism in 1985 with a record number of 14,483,000 visitors coming to Britain during the year. These visitors spent £2,300 m. in accommodation and food and drink alone. Value added tax (VAT) expected to be gained from purchases made by foreign visitors is expected to exceed £600 m. It is estimated by BTA that 4p in every £1 earned by the UK overseas came through tourism. Figure 1.1 shows in diagrammatic form the numbers of tourists in the UK from various parts of the world.

The hotel and catering industry is labour intensive (i.e. it depends on a large work-force) and provides about 10 per cent of the 21 m. jobs in the UK. It is an expanding industry reflecting the growing trends in tourism and leisure activities as well as in conferences and business travel. It is becoming increasingly structured and sophisticated. There are many multinational organisations as well as British companies involved in hotel and catering in the UK. Prospects for jobs are good with an average growth of 2 per cent a year since 1981, the main area of growth being in hotels. Figure 1.2 shows a bar chart of the employment percentages in various sectors of the labour market.

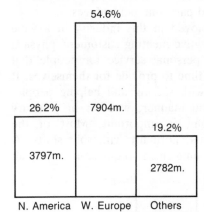

FIG. 1.1 UK Tourist Trade 1985 (*Source*: Dept. of Employment)

In 1984 the Industry employed approximately
2.3 million people spread as follows:

23%	Public services (including educational establishments; NHS, Public administration)
23%	Pubs (includes clubs)
16%	Hotels (including guest houses, hostels and other tourist accommodation)
15%	Catering services (travel catering, retail stores, tourist places)
13%	Restaurants (including cafes, snack-bars, fast food)
5%	Contract catering
5%	Industrial catering (including office catering)

FIG. 1.2 Labour Employment Percentages in the Hotel and Catering Industry

The turnover of staff remains unacceptably high. There are many reasons for this, among which are the industry's traditional low wages and insecurity. Many of the employees (about 50 per cent) are part-time and many more are seasonal (Fig. 1.4). However, with improvements in training structures and technological development as well as regulatory legislation, wages and working conditions have improved. Figures 1.3 and 1.4 show bar charts of the relative percentage of men and women employed in the industry and also the full-time and part-time percentages.

About 2.5 m. people are employed in this industry in a wide range of occupations. All jobs involve meeting customers' physical and social needs. It provides a personal service for people that either cannot or do not have the time to provide for themselves. It is a service industry concerned with serving and helping people. Therefore the right approach and manner, whether in a luxury restaurant or school dining-room, is important. Most of the occupations involve unsocial hours, normally with split shifts. A smart appearance and the use of uniforms is required in nearly all cases.

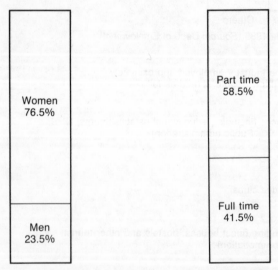

FIG. 1.3 Relative percentages of men and women employed in the Hotel and Catering Industry

FIG. 1.4 Relative percentage of full-time and part-time workers in the Hotel and Catering Industry

Prospects for women in this industry also look good with over 40 per cent of the 450,000 managers, supervisors and proprietors being women. This compares well with the rest of British industry where only about 20 per cent of managers are women. In the non-commercial sector nearly 91 per cent of all employees are women, and in the commercial sector 62 per cent.

The hotel and catering industry is a versatile one. It creates new jobs and provides opportunities for promotion. It also provides many opportunities for enterprising people who wish to be self-employed. Figure 1.5 shows in graphical form the managerial posts available in 1985 for both employed and self-employed managers. Figure 1.6 also compares the relative percentages of employed and self-employed managers in the industry.

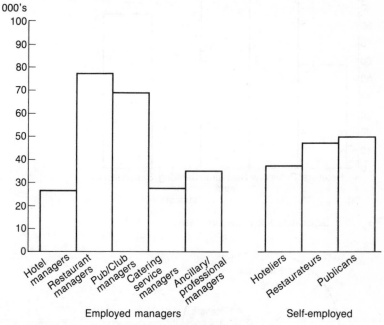

FIG. 1.5 Managers in the Hotel and Catering Industry

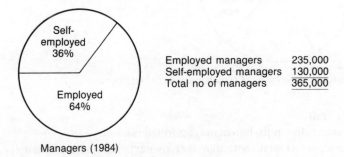

Employed managers	235,000
Self-employed managers	130,000
Total no of managers	365,000

FIG. 1.6 Employed and self-employed managers

The kinds of supervisory and operational staff employed in the industry are listed below, while Figs. 1.7(a),(b) and Figs. 1.8(a),(b) show the numbers employed in the industry in 1985 and their relative percentages.

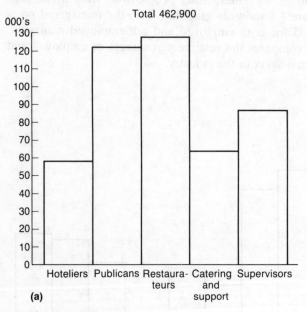

(a)

FIG. 1.7(a) Supervisors and managers (1985)

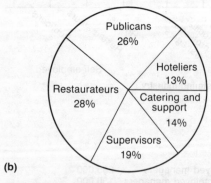

(b)

Fig. 1.7(b) Relative percentages of managerial areas of employment

Supervisory staff

    Publicans (club–pub–bar managers/owners).

    Restaurateurs (restaurant manager/owner; banqueting manager).

Catering and support (canteen/catering personnel; food and beverage manager).

Supervisors (head housekeeper; head barman/woman; head porter; head waiter/waitress).

Operational staff

Food preparation (chefs; cooks; kitchen assistants; counter hands; kitchen porters).

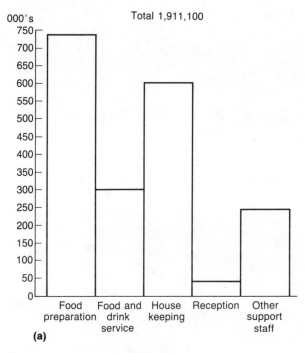

FIG. 1.8(a) Operational staff (1985)

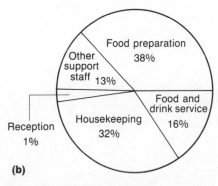

FIG. 1.8(b) Areas requiring staff in percentage terms

Food and drink service (barman/barmaids; waiters/waitresses; dinner ladies; servers).

Housekeeping (chambermaids, valets, school helpers; hospital orderlies).

Reception (receptionists; telephonists; cashiers).

Other support staff (hotel porters; maintenance workers; stores staff).

2

PURCHASING

Careful buying is important to achieve maximum profitability, and therefore all purchasing decisions and procedures require careful thought and strict control. There should be only one person in charge of buying, even if in a large organisation there are assistant buyers. Depending on the size of the establishment this should be either the chef, the food and beverage manager, or a qualified purchasing officer. Usually the head chef is responsible for buying perishable goods. The chef has a specialised knowledge of food requirements and can implement quality control quite speedily and easily. If, however, the chef is not directly responsible then he must have very close liaison with the buyer.

An efficient buyer should:
1. Be well acquainted with products;
2. Know sources of supply;
3. Be able to negotiate prices and conditions;
4. Have some basic legal knowledge related to purchasing.

There are three essential requirements for an efficient purchasing system:
1. Proper purchasing procedures;
2. Clear quality-control mechanisms;
3. Standard purchasing specifications.

PURCHASING PROCEDURES

Before choosing a supplier it is sensible and practical to shop around. This will enable the buyer to compare prices and discounts. The suppliers' minimum order requirements and their delivery procedures can also be identified. It is always important to be aware of the supplier's reputation. Most important, however, is to have information on the quality of the product. The lowest price does not always necessarily mean the cheapest product.

SOURCES OF SUPPLY

There are a number of ways of seeking new sources of supply. At a local level *Yellow Pages* or *Thompsons* should be the starting-point. Trade journals, e.g. *Caterer and Hotelkeeper* or *Hospitality* and trade directories are useful sources of information. Trade exhibitions such as Hotelympia offer an invaluable service updating buyers' knowledge with new developments in the industry. Mail shots from manufacturers and manufacturers' salesmen are also sources of information which will assist the buyer.

INTERNAL ORGANISATION

When a department, e.g. the kitchen, is running low on stocks or a special piece of equipment needs to be bought a purchase requisition (Exhibit 2.1) is sent to the Purchasing Department. The buyer will then write to potential suppliers asking for details about the merchandise to be bought. Small hotels may write an ordinary letter while larger organisations often have standard printed forms. This document is known as a *letter of enquiry*. A letter of enquiry can therefore be defined as a letter or standard form used for requesting information from suppliers about particular products being sought. Sometimes it is quicker or more convenient to make the enquiries by phone. However, details ought to be carefully noted in writing. Larger organisations can communicate with each other by telex or fax.

Upon receipt of letters of enquiry suppliers eager to sell their wares will reply. The reply known as a *quotation* will include details of the merchandise, its quality, size, colour, price, delivery date, any charges, etc. as applicable. The various quotations must be studied carefully in order to select one supplier with whom to place the order.

Having chosen a supplier and having carefully decided on the requirements the *purchase order* (Exhibit 2.2) is placed. An order is another business document which contains the requirements of the buyer and technically requests the supplier to start the delivery process. It is an important document because it starts a legal process placing legal responsibility on both sides. Most establishments use their own standard printed order forms which are signed by an authorised person, are numbered and are normally in duplicate or triplicate. The order will contain the details outlined in the establishment's standard purchasing specification, or as specified in the quotation from the selected supplier.

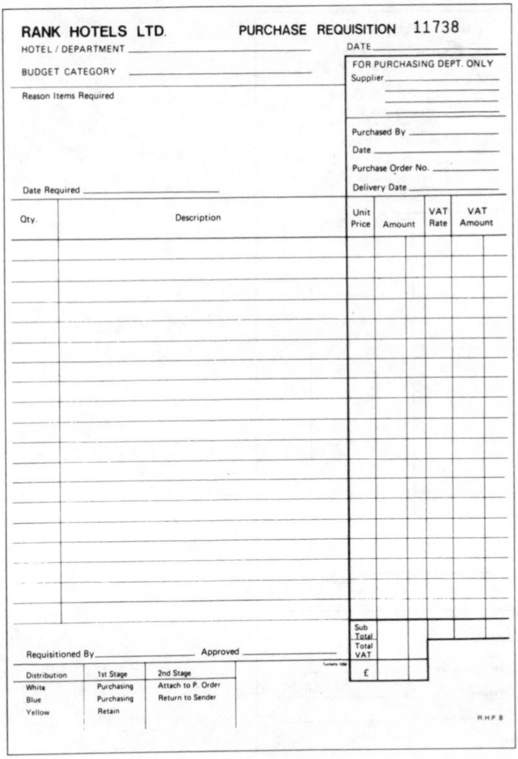

RANK HOTELS LTD. PURCHASE REQUISITION 11738

HOTEL / DEPARTMENT ________ DATE ________

BUDGET CATEGORY ________

FOR PURCHASING DEPT. ONLY
Supplier ________

Reason Items Required

Purchased By ________
Date ________
Purchase Order No. ________
Delivery Date ________

Date Required ________

Qty.	Description	Unit Price	Amount	VAT Rate	VAT Amount

Sub Total
Total VAT
£

Requisitioned By ________ Approved ________

Distribution	1st Stage	2nd Stage
White	Purchasing	Attach to P. Order
Blue	Purchasing	Return to Sender
Yellow	Retain	

R.H.P 8

EXHIBIT 2.1 Purchasing requisition

Daily orders for perishables are usually made by phone and sometimes later confirmed in writing. This is referred to as purchasing by daily market lists (Exhibit 2.3). The quantity to be ordered must be governed by: (1) the storage life of the product; (2) existing stock levels; (3) storage space facilities; (4) expected volume of business; (5) market tendencies; and (6) price stability.

When an order is received the supplier will acknowledge it and confirm delivery details. This is known as an *acknowledgement.* When goods are ready for dispatch an *advice* is sent. This advice, from the supplier to the purchaser, will convey details regarding delivery dates and modes of transport. In these days of escalating costs and postal charges, the acknowledgement and advice are sometimes combined. In the case of food items it is often omitted altogether. The time between ordering and delivering is necessarily so short that the goods are likely to be delivered before the actual acknowledgement/advice note is received. (The procedures outlined above are summarised on Table 2.1.)

Rank Hotels

Rank Hotels Limited
4 Harrington Gardens London SW7 4LH
Telephone (01) 373 8191
Telex 267270

Purchase order

Purchase Order no

70 / 9626

Date

To

Deliver to   ROYAL GARDEN HOTEL
KENSINGTON HIGH STREET
LONDON W8 4PT
Telephone: 01-937 8000

Invoice to   ROYAL GARDEN HOTEL
KENSINGTON HIGH STREET
LONDON W8 4PT
Telephone: 01-937 8000

Quantity	Description	Unit price		Amount	
		£	p	£	p
		Total			
		VAT at standard rate where applicable			
		Totals			

For Rank Hotels Ltd _____   Title _____

This order is subject to the conditions set out overleaf.

Rank Hotels Limited. 4 Harrington Gardens. London SW7 4LH Registered in England No 712215
Registered Office 6 Connaught Place. London W2 2EZ A company within the Rank Organisation

Department _____   Expenditure to date   £ _____

Requisition no _____   This order   £ _____

Budget category code no _____   Uncommitted Balance   £ _____

Distribution
White copy – Supplier   Pink copy – Purchasing dept. file
Yellow copy – Hotel accounts dept   Green copy – Receiving dept

EXHIBIT 2.2 Purchase order

While the availability of suppliers varies with locality, nevertheless the modern caterer has a wide variety of buying methods to
choose from. Small establishments who may have little storage
space and tight cash flows sometimes form a buying consortium
which breaks up bulk purchases and gives members the benefit of
lower prices. Very large organisations like health authorities, large
industrial concerns, major hotel or restaurant groups very often
deal directly with the manufacturer, thus benefiting from lower
prices through bypassing middlemen. When such vast amounts are
involved it is normal practice for the organisation to put its
requirements out to tender. This means they advertise their
requirements for a particular product or group of products.

Suppliers who are able to offer those products bid for the tender
by sending in their quotations. Usually a tender committee meets
to decide which supplier will be offered the contract. (Table 2.2
analyses the various sources of supply.)

Knight's Hotel
MARKET LIST

U	Code	Item	Size	Stock In Hand	On Order	Ordered	Supplier	Quoted Price	Charged Price	No. Received	VDU	Code
	2112	SPRING ONIONS	bunch									2316 PITT
	2113	TOMATOES SALAD M.M.	lb/box									2317 PITT
	2114	TOMATOES BEEF	lb/box									2318 WHI
	2115	TOMATOES CHERRY	lb/box									2319 WHI
	2116	RADDICHIO	tray/lb									2320 PUF
	2117	RADISH	bunch									2321 BUT
	2118	WATERCRESS	box									2322 BUT
	2119	IVY LEAVES	bunch									2323 BUT
	2120	OLIVE LEAVES	bunch									2324 BUT
	2121	OAK SALAD	bunch									2325 BUT
	2122	BLETTE	lb/bunch									2326 BUT
	2123	CHINESE LEAVES	bunch									2327 BRIC
	2124	AVOCADOS	ea/box									2328 MIN
												2329 BUT
	2200	**FRUIT**										2330 COC
	2201	APPLES DESSERT	box/lb									2331 COC
	2202	APPLES COOKING	box/lb									
	2203	BLUEBERRIES	punnet/oz									**2400 DAI**
	2204	BANANAS	lb									2401 MILI
	2205	BLACKCURRANTS	lb/punnet									2402 MILI
	2206	BLACKBERRIES	lb/punnet									2403 CRE
	2207	CHERRIES	lb									2404 CRE
	2208											2405 CRE.
	2209	FIGS	tray/lb									2406 ASS
	2210	GUAVAS	tray/ea									2407 PLAI
	2211	GOOSEBERIES	punnet/lb									2408 BUT
	2212	GRAPEFRUIT PINK	box									2409 BUT
	2213	KIWI FRUIT	ea/tray									2410 EGG
	2214	GRAPES BLACK	box/lb									2411 EGG
	2215	GRAPES WHITE	box/lb									2412 SOU
	2216	GRAPES BLACK ROYAL	box/lb									2413 ICE (
	2217	GRAPES WHITE MUSCAT	box/lb									2414 SOR
	2218	GREENGAGES	tray/lb									2415 CLO
	2219	LEMONS	box									2416 BOL
	2220	LIMES	box/ea									2417 BRIE
	2221	MANDARINES/TANGERINES	lb									2418 FET

EXHIBIT 2.3 Section from a market list

TABLE 2.1 Purchasing procedure (first stage).

	From	To
Requisition	Department	Purchasing officer
Letter of enquiry	Purchasing Officer	Suppliers
Quotation	Suppliers	Purchasing Officer
Order	Purchasing Officer	Selected supplier
Acknowledgement	Supplier	Purchasing Officer
Advice	Supplier	Purchasing Officer

QUALITY CONTROL

Strict control must be exercised over the quality of goods. Quality
control ensures that standards are maintained or if necessary,

improved. By offering the customers the standards they expect, customer satisfaction is achieved. Quality control is a continuous process which starts with the purchasing of commodities and ends with the complete satisfaction of the customer. Money spent on inferior-quality goods is usually money wasted. The reliability of supply is an essential factor to consider. The best supplier is the one who provides the firm with the most efficient service in terms of quality, price and delivery.

TABLE 2.2 Sources of supply.

	Suitability	Advantages	Disadvantages
Manufacturers	Only large concern with contracts	Very competitive prices, deliveries at regular intervals, caterer's own specifications	Costs of storage space, in particular refrigerated space, higher rate of spoilage, capital outlay
Wholesaler	Wide range of non-perishable goods suitable for small, medium-size and large establishments	Free delivery, regular supplies, lower prices, credit facilities	Deliveries may be widely spaced, minimum quantities supplied
Wholesale market	Perishable goods for medium-size establishments	Freshness, choice, quality, low prices	Goods must be collected or delivered paid for
Cash & carry	Non-perishable goods suitable for medium-size establishments	Can choose small quantity at bulk prices	Must arrange own transport. No credit
Local Supplier	Perishable and non-perishable goods for small restaurants and emergencies	Good back-up service also reduces costs in holding stocks	Higher prices, limited choice, unpredictability of supplies and quantities

Many opportunities for dishonesty exist and management must act against these. Bribery of purchaser by suppliers is a particular problem. Some suppliers eager to supply the establishment will offer backhanders (or business incentives, as they are sometimes called) to the buyer. The buyer will supplement his wage with this 'pay-off' which the supplier provides by either inflating the price, substituting a lower-quality product or falsifying delivery notes.

It is important that the establishment has more than one supplier. This minimises the risk of bribery; it ensures continuity of supply and creates competition resulting in keener prices and better quality.

TABLE 2.3 Standard Purchasing Specification.

Product name	How purchased	Specification	Weight
VEAL LOIN	Fresh	Contains 2 rib bones. Flank trim measures 4 inches from outer tip of the loin eye muscle on both the back and leg ends. Fat cover not to exceed $\frac{1}{2}$ inch at leg end.	10–12 lb
POUSSIN SINGLE	English, Grade 1, fresh and eviscerated	Weight to be $\frac{1}{2}$ oz over or under specified weight ordered.	14 oz
MONK FISH	Fresh	Head off	6–8 lb
AUBERGINES	Fresh by the box	$3\frac{1}{2}$ inch to 4 inch diameter. $2\frac{1}{2}$ inch diameter at centre. Slightly oval. Firm stalked. No discolouration.	
TOMATOES	Fresh, by the lb.	Good red colour, mature but not over-ripe or soft. Clean, well developed, well formed, fairly smooth, free from decay, broken skin or internal discolouration. Size: MM $2\frac{1}{4}$ inch in diameter.	12/13 lb box

STANDARD PURCHASING SPECIFICATIONS

Standard Purchasing Specifications state clearly the exact details of what is required. It will be helpful to:

The buyer so that quotations from various suppliers can be examined and compared before selecting the supplier.

The Suppliers because they will be able to prepare accurate quotations in accordance with the buyer's requirements.

The Receiving Clerk as he will know exactly what quality to expect and therefore will reject deliveries that do not comply with the establishments standard specifications.

Standard Purchasing Specifications are invaluable for quality-control purposes as they will ensure consistency throughout. They are particularly useful with regard to the control of food and drink. Food will be ordered in accordance with agreed standards which will have been decided upon after study and testing. Adherence to these standards will ensure that the expected number of portions are obtained because of the consistency in quality. Each establishment defines its own specifications according to its needs. As a general rule, however, they will contain the following information:

1. Definition of goods;
2. Grade or brand name if applicable;
3. Weight, quantity, contents, unit measure, size, colour;
4. Extra information, like country of origin, special preparation, type of packaging, particular cut or process.

Table 2.3 shows examples of Food Standard Purchasing Specifications used by Unifood Inc. for the Sheraton Hotels.

SUMMARY

1. A proper purchasing system is essential to profit and therefore needs strict control.
2. The three essential requirements for successful purchasing are:
   (a)   purchasing procedures;
   (b)   quality control;
   (c)   standard purchasing specifications.
3. It is important to shop around to obtain the best prices and discounts.
4. Purchasing ought to be done by a senior person.

5. Strict control must be exercised over quality.
6. Standard purchasing specifications are essential for precise product requirements.

ASSIGNMENT

1. List the responsibilities of a purchasing officer.
2. Why are standard purchasing specifications prepared?
3. List the advantages and disadvantages of purchasing food from a cash and carry.
4. List sources from which a purchasing officer may obtain information regarding suppliers.
5. List some advantages from attending Hotelympia.
6. Outline the advantages and disadvantages of purchasing direct from a manufacturer.
7. What method of buying perishables and non-perishables are available to a medium-sized restaurant?
8. Prepare a standard purchasing specification for turkeys for a banquet for 560 people.
9. Which document does a supplier send in reply to a letter of enquiry?
10. Prepare a standard purchasing specification for 200 demitasse (cup and plate) for a four-star hotel. They should be white and have a design in blue.
11. 'The lowest price is not always the cheapest.' Explain.
12. Distinguish between an acknowledgement and an advice.

3

RECEIVING DELIVERIES

It would be quite pointless for an organisation to have a strict purchasing procedure if, after having negotiated best prices and agreed terms, no control existed when goods were delivered. It is important, therefore, that goods received comply with goods ordered. Receiving must be seen as an important continuation of the purchasing procedure and therefore careful attention must be given to receiving control to ensure that the quantities, quality and price of goods being delivered corresponds to those ordered.

There are three aspects to receiving which ensure proper control. These are location; personnel; procedures.

LOCATION

A receiving bay should ideally be situated near stores and kitchens to minimise loss and spoilage. It should also be easily accessible from the road to enable delivery vehicles to unload with the minimum inconvenience to traffic. The loading bay should be well lit so that careful checks on the delivery can be carried out. It is essential too that scales are available so that deliveries may be weighed. There should also be a secured storage area for temporary storage of goods. The receiving bay should always be kept clean and free of litter to discourage vermin and avoid contamination.

PERSONNEL

Large organisations employ receiving clerks who are responsible to the purchasing officer and with whom they work closely. Regardless of the size of the establishment the task of receiving should be carried out by trained personnel. Competence and skill in recognising different varieties of food is essential. The person responsible for receiving must be paid a fair wage to avoid the temptation of bribery and allowing inferior and underweight products through. The responsibility of the post which involves signing for thousands of pounds should be reflected in a proper career structure where promotion to food and beverage manager is possible.

PROCEDURES

The receiving clerk needs to organise the day so that deliveries are spread as evenly as possible, thus preventing peak periods. The co-operation of suppliers must be sought for this purpose. It was said earlier that one of the characteristics of a good supplier is a rapid and efficient delivery performance.

All goods delivered are accompanied by a delivery note (Exhibit 3.1) which gives details and quantities. The delivery note ought to be checked with the copy of the order which the delivery clerk must have previously received. This is important so that the purchasing officer or chef is notified of any non-deliveries or variations of the order. Any short deliveries must be noted on the delivery note or on a 'request for credit' (Exhibit 3.2) form, if this available or in use. The delivery man's signature in either case must be obtained. All goods must be thoroughly checked for quality. If there is any doubt the advice of the Purchasing Officer or head chef should be sought. Goods which are unacceptable are returned. A request for credit is prepared and the supplier's driver signs for those goods being returned.

Many establishments keep a 'Goods Received Book' into which all deliveries are entered ('Goods Inwards' or 'Goods Purchased' are alternative names) see Exhibit 3.3. There is no standard design for this. Some may just enter date, supplier's name, order number, delivery note number and any remarks concerning the delivery. Depending on what information is required from the Goods Received Book it may be in the form of an analysis (Exhibit 3.4) where the additional information of the cost of the various commodity headings is included. The information in the Goods

---

Best Catering Supplies Ltd

4 Dopes Road Manchester M4 1LZ

DELIVERY NOTE/ADVICE NOTE

DEL NOTE No: ORDER No: DEL DATE:

DELIVER TO: _____

EXHIBIT 3.1 Delivery note/Advice note

Received Book is useful to the Buying Office to check purchases as well as the Accounts Department who must pay the suppliers for the goods delivered. By analysing deliveries it is possible to identify the costs of goods by groups of commodities.

Those establishments that do not use a Goods Received Book question its usefulness and argue that the effort, time and cost involved heavily outweigh any merit its use may have.

After delivery, an invoice (Exhibit 3.5) is sent by post by the supplier, although for speed and to avoid postal charges many suppliers send the invoice at the time of delivery. The invoice lists all goods supplied and their charges. It records any trade discounts and the amount, if any, of VAT charged. Once an invoice has been issued it ought not to be altered physically and any discrepancy is rectified with the use of credit (Exhibit 3.6) and debit notes. The Accounts Office will check the delivery note and invoice, but it would be useful if the receiving clerk also did so. A *credit* note *decreases* the amount owed by the purchaser and the *debit* note *increases* the amount. Credit notes are usually printed in red to distinguish them from other documents. All transactions regarding

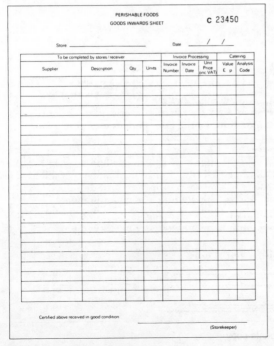

EXHIBIT 3.2 Request for credit

EXHIBIT 3.3 Goods inward sheet

GOODS RECEIVED SHEET – FOOD

0733

Day: Date:

SUPPLIER	DELIVERY NOTE No.	DRY STORES	COMMODITY ANALYSIS – WET STOCK							V.A.T.	TOTAL	ACCOUNTS OFFICE – INVOICE DETAILS			
			MEAT	FISH	POULTRY	FRUIT/VEG.	DAIRY	BREAD	Sub Total Wet Stock			AMOUNT	DIFFERENCE	G.R.S. REF.	INV. No.

Prepared by: Checked by:

EXHIBIT 3.4 Goods received sheet

FITCH & SON LTD
Wholesale Catering Supplies

By appointment to Her Majesty the Queen Provision Merchants Fitch & Son Ltd London

FITCH & SON LTD
INC BERNARD & CO(HARROW RD)LTD
78 SILVERTHORNE ROAD
LONDON SW8 3HJ
SALES 720-0051 ADMIN 720-1660

V.A.T. REG NO 235-8852-36
INVOICE/ACCOUNTS COPY

NORMAL DELIVERY
MON 00
TUE 32
WED 00
THU 32
FRI 00

GOODS TO
INSTITUTE OF CIVIL ENGINEERING
1 GT GEORGE ST
LONDON SW1
DELS TO REAR OF BLDG
222-7722 144

COUNTRY RANGE

IN CASE OF QUERY PLEASE QUOTE	OUR ORDER REF.	ACCOUNT No.	REP	ROUND No.	DELIVERY INSTRUCTIONS/ CUSTOMER REFERENCE	DATE	PAGE No.
INVOICE No. 335412	988167	018292	I	32	NOT BETWEEN NOON & 3PM V	22/05/87	1 OF 1

QTY.	PACK DESCRIPTION	PRODUCT DESCRIPTION	PRODUCT CODE	WEIGHT	UNIT	UNIT PRICE	VALUE	VAT CODE	ITEM No
1	12X1 KG	SALSIFY	26101		CASE	14.650	14.65	A	1
1	12X1 KG	FLAGEOLET BEANS	31114		CASE	10.690	10.69	A	2
12	* X14 OZ	STRAWBERRIES IN SYRUP	10735		EACH	0.720	8.64	A	3
1	24X12 OZ	ASPARAGUS SPEARS GREEN MILNES	10758		CASE	31.350	31.35	A	4
1	6XA10	BEETROOT SLICED COUNTRY RANGE	10889		CASE	7.460	7.46	A	5
12	* X14 OZ	PIMIENTOES IRIS CRO	11119		EACH	0.580	6.96	A	6
1	6X3 KG	TOMATOES PLUM CHOICE SPANISH	24585		CASE	7.150	7.15	A	7
	6X1800 GR	TUNA FISH IN OIL R.CROWN	25967	TEMPORARILY OUT OF STOCK, PLEASE REORDER					
1	* X3 KG	SULTANAS	18619		EACH	4.730	4.73	A	9
2	2X.5 GAL	BRANSTON PICKLE	34848		CASE	8.950	17.90	A	10
1	2X.5 GAL	S HORSERADISH CREAMED BURGESS	16390		CASE	8.460	8.46	A	11
1	4X1 KG	QUAKER GARLIC CROUTONS	30855		CASE	13.650	13.65	A	12
	4X1 KG	QUAKER CHEESE&HERB CROUTONS	65548	TEMPORARILY OUT OF STOCK, PLEASE REORDER					

****************** SHORTAGES AND RETURNS ******************

INV NO	LN/CDE	DESCRIPTION	QTY	REASON

VAT %	A= ZERO	
GOODS	131.66	131.66
DISC	6.64-	6.64-
SUBTOT	125.02	125.02
VAT		0.00
TOTAL		125.02

ORDERS are accepted for goods subject to availability. PRICES are quoted subject to market fluctuations and the price charged is that ruling at the time of delivery
DELIVERIES must be checked in the presence of the driver and CLAIMS for loss or damage cannot be entertained unless signed for accordingly
CLAIMS on perishable goods must be made within 3 days, other goods within 1 month. ACCOUNTS must be settled by the 15th of the month following the month of delivery
SHRINKAGE of 1% has been allowed for in the price of items sold by weight

EXHIBIT 3.5 Invoice/Accounts copy

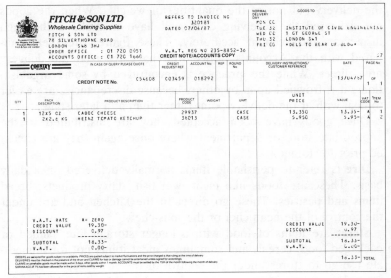

EXHIBIT 3.6 Credit note

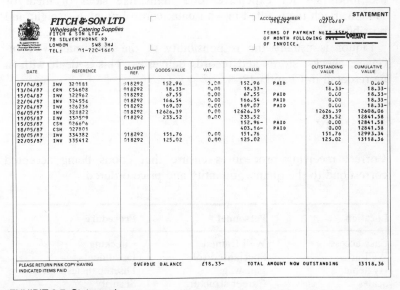

EXHIBIT 3.7 Statement

receipt of goods and payment for them can be verified when the supplier sends in a statement (Exhibit 3.7).

Many establishments have introduced a system of **blind receiving**. The purpose of this system is to ensure that strict control of the receipt of goods is exercised. The receiving clerk is notified of the delivery but not of the quantities or weights. When the goods are delivered the receiving clerk will have to make a thorough inspection and account accurately. These figures are then compared with the Accounts Office who have received the delivery note direct. While this practice is encouraged by some organisations, it is frowned upon by others because discrepancies are easier to deal with at the delivery point rather than at a later stage.

Once goods have been accepted they are distributed to the appropriate store or department where once again they are checked prior to storage.

Directs refer to perishable items normally delivered on a daily basis. These are foods like meat, wet fish, dairy products, bread items and pastries. These go direct to the kitchen and are under the control of the head chef or the sous-chef.

Stores are items of food with a longer storage life. Tinned or packaged food, cereals and sometimes meat joints not for immediate use go to stores under the control of the storekeeper who will issue them to the kitchen at some later date. Many establishments use food tags for expensive food items like sides of meat or salmon. Each tag is filled in with date, control number, weight and possibly price.

Liquor is usually the responsibility of the cellarman who receives, checks, stores and records deliveries. This is dealt with in more detail in Chapter 12.

SUMMARY

Correct receiving procedures ensure that goods being accepted correspond to the quality, quantity and price ordered.

Location	Personnel	Procedure
Easy access	Well trained	Checking
Well lit	Specialised role	Documents
Hygienic	Fair wage	Discrepancies
Scales	Career structure	Security

ASSIGNMENT

1. What points should you consider when planning a goods receiving area?

2. What action would you take if you discover short delivery?
3. Why is 'delivery performance' important?
4. What qualities would you seek in a goods receiving clerk?
5. Why do purchasing orders have more than one copy?
6. What is meant by 'blind receiving'?
7. How can a receiving clerk avoid pilfering taking place?
8. Explain the procedures once goods have been received and accepted.
9. To whom is the goods receiving clerk responsible?
10. Why is the delivery note matched with the order form?
11. What action should a receiving clerk take if shoulders of lamb are delivered at 98p per lb when in fact they were ordered at 58p per lb?
12. A delivery is made late on Friday afternoon of dairy products, but the delivery-man has misplaced the delivery note. What should the receiving clerk do?
13. Fill in the following boxes concerning movements of documents. The first one is already done.

	From:	To:
Letter of enquiry	Buyer	Seller
Quotation		
Order		
Acknowledgement		
Advice		
Delivery note		
Request for credit		
Credit note		

From:	To:

Debit note

Invoice

Statement

4

STORES AND STORES CONTROL

INTRODUCTION

Storage space in catering establishments is generally limited in size and is an expensive overhead. It is not a direct revenue earner, in the same way as the restaurant; therefore it is essential that it is used efficiently. The stores, although not a revenue earner itself, is nevertheless, necessary because it services the production area.

Stores are essential in any catering establishment so that the risk of running short of any commodity is eliminated. A properly organised store helps to reduce loss through wastage or pilfering. Stores that are run in an orderly and efficient manner are an aid to profitability since stocks can be kept at the correct level and condition.

SECURITY

Spoilage and pilferage of goods while in stores are prime causes of increased costs. Tight security is necessary to protect the stocks from loss through pilfering. Goods received and issued must be properly handled and accounted for. Locks to the stores must be strong. Keys must be kept by the storeman and the food and beverage manager only. No one should be allowed into the store without authorisation and a counter at the entrance can prevent unauthorised entry. The stores should operate at specified hours and issues outside these times should be discouraged. Adequate lighting, whether natural or electrical, is essential for identification of goods and for safety as well as security reasons.

HYGIENE

The stores should be away from direct sunshine so that it is cool at all times. It should therefore preferably face north. Adequate ventilation is necessary to provide the correct temperature and humidity so that the life of food can be maximised. High levels of humidity creates dampness which encourages bacteria to grow, ruins packaged food and rusts tins.

Mobile adjustable shelving racks of stainless steel, if possible, would allow flexibility when changing the layout of the stores. They should be easy to dismantle and to clean and must always be raised 457 mm from the floor. For perishable goods shelves should be slatted to allow free circulation of air. All food must be stored at least 500 mm away from walls, windows and ventilators.

Care must be given to storing food in adequate containers to prevent attacks by insects and vermin and to avoid strong smells being absorbed by other foods. Heavy bins containing dry goods, like pulses or granular foods should have wheels for ease of movement for cleaning.

Blown tins, i.e. when the ends bulge, must be thrown away or returned to the suppliers if this is possible. It is dangerous to consume food from blown tins as bacteria-contaminated food can cause food poisoning. Dented tins ought to be used as soon as possible because the dent will cause rust which will eventually puncture the tin.

A very high standard of hygiene is essential for health reasons and to avoid accumulation of dirt. Cleanliness in stores will discourage insects and vermin. (There is more on hygiene in Chapter 14.)

LAYOUT

Stores should be conveniently positioned between the receiving area and the production area. This minimises loss and damage, speeds storage and issue routine and cuts down labour time. The stores should have ample storage space but not be so big as to encourage overstocking and wasteful use of expensive floor space. It should be well laid out to provide facilities for the various types of stock items. Whenever possible refrigerated and deep-freeze stores should be near dry stores so that delivery and control can be simplified. The storekeeper's office should be located in the area so that all movements can be easily identified by him. Weighing machines should be available.

Correct temperatures are necessary to prolong the life of food and to prevent over-ripening. The inside flesh of apples, for example, will turn brown if chilled at too low a level. In

Appendix 2 some useful storage temperatures are given, but it would be best to consult a catering theory book for accurate storage temperatures of individual commodities.

DOCUMENTATION

The three main documents used in a stores to maintain proper control of stocks are:

1. Bin card;
2. Stock card (or stores ledger card);
3. Requisition form.

These are necessary so that accurate records are kept of goods coming in and going out of stores, i.e. *receipts* and *issues*. It enables the storeman to check stock and ordering levels and provides management with a valuation of stocks. The bin card and stock card are really duplicate information. They may be used together for tighter control in large establishments. To keep both systems in a small establishment may well be unnecessary because of the cost in administering the system itself.

BIN CARDS

A bin card (Exhibit 4.1) is prepared for every commodity in the store and for every size if there are different sizes of the same commodity. It simply shows the balance of the item in stock. It records receipts and issues and date of every transaction. It is good practice for it to show the minimum stock level of the particular commodity so that reordering may be done. Normally, the bin card is kept on the shelf against the item it refers to.

STOCK CARDS

A stock card (Exhibit 4.2), sometimes referred to as a stores ledger card, serves basically the same purpose as a bin card. It differs, however, in that as well as movements in the quantity of stocks it also records movements in the value of the stocks. Because it shows the value of stocks it is a useful aid to stocktaking and valuing stocks. Smaller establishments dispense with this because of the work involved and some probably keep stock cards for very expensive items only.

EXHIBIT 4.1 Bin card

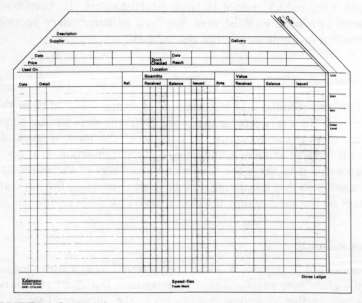

EXHIBIT 4.2 Stock card

REQUISITION FORM

The purpose of a requisition form (Exhibit 4.3) is to obtain goods from the stores. The requisition form must therefore be signed by an authorised person. Good practice encourages departments to send in requisitions once a day so that stricter control of movements of stock can be kept. Extra requisition for small items should not be encouraged. A requisition form shows stocks already held by the department so as to avoid unnecessary stocks being requested. Every requisition form must be clearly completed with quantity and date. On receipt of an authorised requisition form the storekeeper will issue the goods. All issues must be carefully counted and weighed.

Royal Garden Hotel

STORES REQUISITION SHEET

9202

DEPARTMENT

DATE

QTY.	UNITS	DESCRIPTION	UNIT COST £	UNIT COST p	TOTAL COST £	TOTAL COST p
		TOTAL				

AUTHORISED BY	ISSUED BY	RECEIVED BY

RGH 14

EXHIBIT 4.3 Requisition form

INVENTORY

Some establishments keep a moving inventory system with every item within a commodity range on one sheet (see Fig. 4.1). One of the advantages of this system is that it makes costing items easier. Another advantage is that it simplifies the valuation of stock when stock-taking. It also saves time having to look through cards to obtain information. Its main advantage is that because of its compact set-up it gives ready information and provides a good measure of control with the minimum of paperwork.

This system can be combined with an order form so that after checking of levels against the minimum level column, an order column can be completed. This again minimises and streamlines paperwork.

Fruit and veg(4)

Stock No.	Item	(1) Opening stock (lb)	(2) Receipts (lb)	(3) OS Rec	(4) Issues (lb) 1	Issues (lb) 2	Issues (lb) 3	(5) Total issues	(6) CS (lb)	(7) Price £ p	(8) Value £ p
24/1	Aubergine	24	8	32	26	5	–	31	1	0 80	0 80
24/2	Artichoke										
24/3	Apples	CS from last sheet	From delivery		From requisition	From requisition	From requisition				
24/4	Bananas										
24/5	Carrots										

Optional (used only for OS or CS for cost of goods sold start/end period)

(1) Opening stocks are the closing stocks from previous sheet.
(2) Receipts refer to what has been received on that day.
(3) OS + Rec is the total of the opening stock plus receipts.
(4) Issues are what is issued to different departments.
(5) Total issues is equal to the amount in each issue column added together.
(6) Closing stock (CS) is the difference of OS + Rec less total issues.
(7) Price is the current price.
(8) Value is the amount of closing stock times the price.

FIG. 4.1 Inventory sheet

SUMMARY

1. Stores are essential to prevent shortage of materials.
2. Food items are particularly vulnerable to pilferage. Security must therefore be strict.
3. Hygiene standards in stores must be high to prevent spoilage and contamination of food.
4. Stores take up expensive floor space, therefore layout must be carefully planned and economically used.
5. Documentation in stores is necessary for control purposes.
6. The principal documents are: (1) bin card; (2) stock card; (3) requisition form.

ASSIGNMENT

1. List the points you consider necessary for the siting of stores.
2. Explain why stores are essential to a catering establishment.
3. Why should stores preferably face north?
4. Explain how dampness can affect the value of stocks.
5. List security measures needed for control and storage of food, cleaning materials or equipment.
6. Why should overstocking be discouraged?

The information set out below assignment 8 has been obtained from stores. You are to prepare:

7. (a)   A *bin card* for every commodity on the list.
   (b)   Enter current stock balance.
   (c)   By entering daily receipts and issues you must calculate the current balance on every bin card.
8. (a)   A *stock card* for every commodity on the list.
   (b)   Enter current stock balance and value.
   (c)   By entering daily receipts you must calculate the current balance on every stock card.

Commodity	Unit	Package	Current stock (balance)	Price per unit at (£):
Tea-bags	100's	pkt	28	1.02 per pkt
Cornflakes	500 g	pkt	24	0.85 per pkt
Macaroni	7 lb	bag	29 lb	1,82 per bag
Apricots	A2	tin	35	0.63 per tin
Peaches	A4	tin	42	1.60 per tin
Baked beans	A2	tin	24	0.49 per tin
Tomato purée	5 kg	tin	8	2.85 per tin
Vanilla essence		bot.	16	1.42 per bot
Cayenne pepper	250 g	pkt	11	0.75 per pkt
Honey		portions	62	0.07 per portion
Rice	50 kg	bag	220 kg	38.20 per bag
Sugar-cubes		pkt	16	0.52 per pkt

May 1: *Received:* 78 teas at £1.04; 30 vanillas at £1.45; 36 sugars at 54p; 10 apricots at 63p; 20 peaches at £1.59; 4 peppers at 75p

Issued: 6 teas; 5 cornflakes; 22 lb macaroni; 1 apricot; 3 peaches; 2 tomato purée; 36 honeys

May 2: *Received:* 30 cornflakes at 87p; macaroni 4 bags at £1.80; baked beans 10 at 50p; tomato purée 3 × 5 kg at £2.80; honey 104 at 84p

Issued: 6 teas; 5 cornflakes; 15 lb macaroni; 2 apricots; 1 tomato purée; 48 honeys; 1 cayenne

May 3: *Received:* 24 sugars at 52p; 1 bag rice at £38.30; 20 teas at £1.03; 6 cornflakes at 86p; 10 apricots at 64p; 4 peaches at £1.61

Issued: 10 teas; 6 cornflakes; 20 lb macaroni; 6 apricots; 6 peaches; 36 honeys; 25 kg rice

May 4: *Received:* 5 bags macaroni at £1.83

Issued: 6 teas; 5 cornflakes; 8 lb macaroni; 1 apricot; 2 peaches; 6 baked beans; 52 honeys; 16 sugars; 41 kg rice

PART II

0.0080769

104 at 0.84p.

5

DISH COSTING

Often one hears people saying that such a footballer did not play up to standard or that so and so's behaviour is not up to standard. In other words 'standard' is a level of measurement, that is, a means by which something can be measured or judged against something else. In costing, standards are essential as part of the system of control. These 'standard costs' are determined by:

Standard recipes (the ingredients used in preparing a dish).
Standard portions (the size of the portion served).

STANDARD RECIPES

These contain the written instructions for producing food or units of beverage of a certain quality and of particular quantities. This is determined after frequent and accurate testing.

It will list the quantities of ingredients and will also give instructions on methods of preparation and presentation. This will ensure that every time the same dish or cocktail is prepared, no matter by whom, it will always result in both the same quantity and quality. This is a useful aid to portion control as it will give the number and size of portions that can be obtained. It will also be possible to cost the food more exactly and therefore order the raw materials more accurately. The customers benefit from being served a consistent product.

How or where standard recipes are compiled depends very much on the particular establishment. A small restaurant, for example, may keep them in a copybook. A large establishment with a large number of cooks may keep a sophisticated recipe manual which is periodically updated. With the ever-increasing use of computers in catering, some establishments will have computerised standard recipes. The main advantage of the computerised recipe is the cost of the dish which is automatically updated every time there is a change in the price of an ingredient. There are establishments which have their standard recipes on the wall accompanied by colour photographs of the finished dish to assist with the presentation.

RECIPE FOR *Eclac Au fuist du Jour*			WINSTONS HOTEL LIMITED					

QUANTITY PRODUCED ___10___ PORTIONS   CODE No. ☐☐☐☐

PORTION SIZE _____   RESTAURANT "ANDROMEDA"·

PORTION SIZE _____   _____

UNIT	INGREDIENTS	DATE		DATE		DATE		DATE	
		AT	AMOUNT	AT	AMOUNT	AT	AMOUNT	AT	AMOUNT
150g	Flour	0.14 lb	0.05						
6	Eggs	0.06 ea	0.36						
1/4 L	Milk	0.23 pt	0.10						
100g	Butter	0.97 lb	0.21						
200ml	Double cream	1.23 pt	0.11						
5 No.	Kiwis	0.16 ea	0.80						
5 No.	Bananas	0.48 lb	0.96·						
5 Punnets	Raspberries	2.25 pnt	11.25						
100g	Icing Sugar	2.23 per 2kg	0.07						
2 Punnets	Strawberries	0.35 pnt	0.70						
	TOTAL COST		14.61						
	COSTPERPORTION		1.46						

EXHIBIT 5.1 Recipe sheet

Whatever system is used the standard recipe (Exhibit 5.1) must show a name with possibly a recipe number. It will list the ingredients together with the quantities required. The expected yield, that is, the number of portions possible, will be shown and the method of preparation and production listed by stages. If it is being used as a dish-costing sheet (Exhibit 5.2), then it has a dual purpose, in which case the current price of each ingredient and the unit cost will be shown next to each ingredient. In many instances the price columns are multiples so that whenever changes in price occur these are shown and can be compared with previous price changes. The total cost of the dish will be shown as well as the cost per portion.

The most accurate way of finding the cost of a dish is by costing all its ingredients. The selling price of the dish can later be fixed in accordance with the profit the caterer is seeking to make. We have seen that a recipe card can also be used for costing the dish. Another alternative is to prepare a dish-costing card/sheet which excludes method of preparation and production and simply concentrates on pricing. There are as many varieties of recipe cards and dish-costing cards as there are establishments. Every establishment finds a system suitable to its operation. Non-computerised establishments cannot alter costed dishes immediately every time there is a price change, so some prepare new costings only when prices have changed substantially. Others allow a percentage for price increases and check this periodically.

INGREDIENTS	QTY	UNIT	UNIT VALUE	TOTAL VALUE	UNIT VALUE	TOTAL VALUE	UNIT VALUE	TOTAL VALUE	UNIT VALUE	TOTAL VALUE	UNIT VALUE	TOTAL VALUE
TOTAL COST												
SELLING PRICE												
PROFIT												
COST OF SALES %												

EXHIBIT 5.2 Dish-costing sheet

STANDARD PORTIONS

The size of the portion, that is, the amount of any item that will be served every time the item is ordered, is the most important standard that management must set. The standard portion is the fixed quantity a customer receives in return for the selling price.

Standard portions help to control costs, and also stop variations in the gross profit (see Ch. 7). Apart from more efficient control it reduces customer discontent since no customer is treated more favourably than another. Animosity among kitchen staff and restaurant personnel is often caused when one preferred waiter receives larger portions for his customers than do the others. As standard portion means equal amount, this problem is eliminated.

The unit cost of a portion is found by dividing the total cost of the recipe by the number of standard portions that the recipe yields. For example, a recipe for steak and kidney pie for four may be costed at £2.30. By dividing by 4 (2.30/4 = 57.5p) the cost of the portion is obtained. From the cost of the standard portion the selling price is obtained by calculating the gross profit percentage which must be sufficient to cover the many overheads of the business. The selling price is dealt with in Chapter 10 and for the moment we must concentrate on costing the ingredients of the dish.

PRICES

The unit price for costing ingredients is obtained either from the suppliers' invoices or from the dry stores. In larger organisations prices are obtainable from the Purchasing Office. The following prices have been obtained for the recipe at Fig. 5.1.

Chicken	at £0.52 per lb	Paprika	at £0.32 per 25 g
Onions	at £0.12 per lb	Red wine	at £2.75 per litre
Garlic	at £1.20 per lb	Tomato	at £0.80 per lb
Unsalted butter	at £1.00 per lb	Arrowroot	at £0.52 per lb
Flour	at £0.12 per lb		

EXAMPLE

Prepare a costing sheet for Chicken in Red Wine. Calculate the cost per portion.

Calculation
Chicken: $3 \times 52 = 156$ p

Onions $\dfrac{2.5}{16} \times 12 = 1.875$ p

Garlic: approx. weight 0.94 oz
approx. 14 cloves per garlic

$\dfrac{0.94}{16} \times 120 = 7.050$ p

$\dfrac{7.050}{14} = 0.504$ p

Butter: $\dfrac{1.5}{16} \times 100 = 9.375$ p

Flour: $\quad \dfrac{1}{16} \times 12 = 0.750$ p

Paprika: $\quad \dfrac{1}{25} \times 32 = 1.280$ p

Wine: $\quad$ (1.76 pints = 1 litre)
$\qquad$ 1.76 pints cost £2.75
$\qquad \frac{1}{2}$ pint costs $\dfrac{0.5}{1.76} \times 275 = 78.125$ p

Tomato: $\quad \dfrac{1}{1} \times 80 = 80$ p

Arrowroot: $\quad$ (1 oz = 28.35 g)
$\qquad$ 16 oz = 453.6 g
$\qquad$ 453.6 g costs 52 p
$\qquad$ 1 g costs $\dfrac{1}{453.6} \times 52 = 0.115$ p

FIG. 5.1 Recipe

| **Dish:** Chicken with wine | | **Recipe No:** 24 | | |
| **No. of portions:** 4 | | **Cost per portion:** 82.256 p | | |

Ingredients	Unit price (£)	Unit measure	Quantity	Cost* (p)
Chicken	0.52	lb	3 lb	156.000
Onions	0.12	lb	$2\frac{1}{2}$ oz	1.875
Garlic	1.20	lb	1 clove	0.504
Unsalted butter	1.00	lb	$1\frac{1}{2}$ oz	9.375
Flour	0.12	lb	1 oz	0.750
Paprika	0.32	25 g	1 g	1.280
Red Wine	2.75	litre	$\frac{1}{2}$ pint	78.125
Salt/pepper	–	–	To taste	1.000
Tomatoes	0.80	lb	1 lb	80.000
Arrowroot	0.52	lb	1 g	0.115

$$\dfrac{\text{Quantity} \times \text{Unit price}}{\text{Unit measure}} = \text{Cost} \qquad \text{Total cost} \qquad 329.024 \text{ p}$$

Note: Cost per portion 81.917 (in pence and part of a penny) = 329.024 ÷ 4

Small operators would probably find that the calculation above, costed to the nearest penny, would be sufficient. An acceptable costing for Fig. 5.1 above would be:

$$156$$
$$2$$
$$0$$
$$9$$
$$1$$
$$1$$
$$78$$
$$1$$
$$80$$
$$\underline{0}$$
$$328$$

$$\frac{328}{4} = 82 \text{ p per portion.}$$

However, those establishments using computers would have much more accurate costings in line with that given on the example recipe card above. Large chain outlets, in particular those specialising in volume fast food would need to be very accurate. It is important, therefore, when costing dishes to build in notional allowances for ingredients right down to minor items like herbs, the cost of which can mount up over the course of a year.

SUMMARY

1. The advantages of a standard recipe are:
   (a)   consistency in preparation;
   (b)   aid to portion control;
   (c)   assists in accurate purchasing;
   (d)   customer satisfaction.
2. The form these recipes take depends on the size of the establishment.
3. The actual cost of a dish is determined by accurately costing all its ingredients.
4. The unit cost of a portion is achieved by dividing the cost of the dish by the expected number of portions.
5. A dish-costing sheet contains cost of ingredients.
6. A standard recipe contains cost of ingredients together with instructions on preparation and cooking.
7. Standard portion is a fixed amount of food served.
8. The standard portion is determined by management according to the establishment's pricing policy.

9. The advantages of standard portions are:
   (a)   helps control costs;
   (b)   reduces variations in gross profit;
   (c)   reduces customer discontent;
   (d)   eliminates staff animosity.

ASSIGNMENT

From your cookery textbook obtain recipes for the following. Using the price list below *prepare* a costing sheet, *enter* all details and *calculate* the cost of each ingredient accurately. *Cost* the dish then *find* the cost per portion.

Genoese sponge
Victoria sandwich
Scones
Poulette en cocotte
Fricassee de volaille

Escalope de veau à la crème
Fricassee de veau
Boeuf braise
Filet de sole véronique
Homard Americaine

PRICE LIST

Meat

Topside	£1.76 per lb
Thick flank	£1.70 per lb
Stewing beef	£1.34 per lb
Veal (shoulder or breast)	£0.85 per lb
Veal escalope	£3.94 per lb

Fish

Lobster	£4.75 per lb
Sole	£2.00 per lb

Groceries

Tomato purée	£0.80 per lb
Cayenne pepper	£1.10 per 8 oz
Salt	£0.06 per lb
Flour	£0.12 per lb
Baking powder	£0.52 per lb

Fats and Oils

Oil	£0.57 per litre
Dripping	£0.28 per lb

Vegetables

Carrots	£0.10 per lb
Garlic	£2.00 per lb
Celery	£0.45 per lb
Lemon	£0.08 each
Parsley	£0.20 bunch
Onions	£0.10 per lb
Shallots	£1.20 per lb
Tomatoes	£0.80 per lb

Dairy

Butter	£1.00 per lb
Cream–double	£0.76 per pint
Cream–single	£0.56 per pint
Eggs	£0.60 per dozen
Margarine	£0.48 per lb
Milk	£0.23 per pint

Beverages

Brandy	£7.58 per bot.
Sherry	£2.31 per bot.
Wine–white	£2.75 per litre

Stocks

Meat	£0.40 per gallon
Fish	£0.20 per gallon
Bouquet garni	£1.45 per 20

Fruit

Grapes–white	£1.20 per lb

6

WASTAGE AND YIELD

WASTAGE

A certain amount of waste in catering is inevitable. This amount of waste is of real concern to management since the degree of wastage provides an indication of the efficiency of the enterprise. In a control cycle there are four areas in which wastage may occur.

WASTAGE IN STORES

A minimal amount of waste can occur while goods are in storage. Leakages, spillages, breakages, and in the case of beverages through ullage also. Some of the waste may be accidental, other waste is produced through bad purchasing or overstocking causing deterioration in food. Excessive or regular losses in stores through wastage must be remedied.

WASTAGE IN PREPARATION

After buying 20 lb of chuck steak or 15 lb of plaice for example, it does not follow that the same weight of meat and fish will be served. In fact, in the case of this particular fish only about half the weight will be served; the rest will be waste. Experience and skill is therefore required so that the right weight is ordered thus preventing shortages or excess food. There are certain and un-avoidable losses in the preparation of food, but vigilance is necessary to ensure that waste is contained within an acceptable percentage of the food purchased. An average size crab or lobster will produce only between 30 and 35 per cent of its original weight. Fish like plaice or sole may lose as much as 50 per cent of its original weight, whereas fish like cod, bream or salmon will produce over 70 per cent edible weight. Fruits and vegetables can have a loss of between 3 and 60 per cent during preparation depending on their quality and degree of ripeness. Everybody knows the story of the young commis who, having switched on the electric peeler, found potatoes the size of marbles upon his return from a quick smoke and cuppa! An example of preparation loss!

WASTAGE DURING COOKING

Loss through shrinkage is the main cause of wastage in the cooking process. Over-cooking and very high temperatures reduce weight unnecessarily, thus either reducing the portion size or reducing the number of portions possible. Roasting joints generally lose between 30 and 40 per cent.

PLATE WASTE

This term describes food left on the plate by the customer. It is related to customer satisfaction and waste must be monitored to ensure it stays at an acceptable level. Excessive plate waste may be attributed to many factors, and if it occurs regularly its cause must be determined. It could mean that portions are too large and therefore a reduction in portion size is possible accompanied by a corresponding reduction in selling price.

The waste could be due to bad service by waiting staff who may not have trimmed the food properly, or not served it in an appetising manner, or served it cold when it should have been hot. The food could have been of inferior quality when purchased or it could have been badly cooked. All these give rise to waste and cause for concern. The reasons ought to be identified and rectified immediately.

YIELD

Either at work or college the expression 'the standard yield is' must have been used more than once. 'The yield of a joint of meat' means the amount of edible or usable meat in the joint, that is, the amount which, after trimming and cooking, remains for serving to customers. In other words, the yield is the number of acceptable portions that can be served from a prepared and cooked joint of meat, fish, vegetable or indeed any item of food or drink. Earlier we discussed the uses of standard recipes. Standard recipes enable us to estimate the yield. If the standard recipe is followed strictly then the standard yield is achieved and consequently the expected number of standard portions will be served.

The yield is therefore the usable or edible weight available from a raw item. The price of course alters. The unit cost of usable weight is higher than the unit cost of the original weight, unit cost being the price per lb. For example, if a joint of meat weighing 10 lb costs £2.25 per lb, the cost of that joint would be £22.50. If after preparation and cooking that joint has been reduced to 6 lb one cannot say that the price per pound is still £2.25; 6 lb at £2.25 equals £13.50 yet the original price paid was £22.50. The £9.00 difference (£22.50 − £13.50) must be reflected in the price per portion. Once the standard portion size is known it is possible to calculate the cost per portion and we shall see from the example following below how this can be achieved.

It is possible therefore to calculate:

1. Cost of raw (or original) weight;
2. Waste and trimmings weight;
3. Percentage of waste;
4. Usable weight;
5. Percentage of usable weight;
6. Cost of usable weight;
7. Cost per standard portion.

EXAMPLE

A York ham bought on the bone weighed 13 lb 6 oz and cost £2.32 per lb. Bones, fat and trim amounted to 2 lb 8 oz. Work out the seven calculations listed above.

1. *Cost of raw weight*
   13 lb 6 oz at £2.32 per lb
   To avoid confusion later bring all the weights to ounces,

   $(13 \times 16 = 208 + 6 = 214 \text{ oz})$
   $$\frac{214 \times 2.32}{16} = £31.03$$
   1 oz costs 0.145 p

2. *Weight of trimmings and waste* (these are either physically weighed or the usable weight is deducted from the raw or the original weight)
   Bone, fat and trim
   = 2 lb 8 oz = 40 oz

3. *Percentage of waste*
   $$= \frac{\text{Waste weight}}{\text{Raw weight}} \times \frac{100}{1}$$
   $$= \frac{40}{214} \times \frac{100}{1} = 18.69\%$$

4. *Usable weight* (this is obtained either by physically weighing the food or by deducting the waste weight from the raw weight)
214 − 40 = 174 oz

5. *Percentage of usable weight*

$$= \frac{\text{Usable weight}}{\text{Raw weight}} \times \frac{100}{1}$$

$$= \frac{174}{214} \times \frac{100}{1} = 81.31\%$$

6. *Cost of usable weight*
The cost of the usable weight is still the same as that of the original weight. Even though the weight is now less, the purchase price paid does not alter. The purchase price (cost) of the original weight was estimated at 0.145 per oz. The purchase price (cost) of the weight is therefore
174 oz cost £31.03
1 oz cost $\dfrac{31.03}{174} = 0.178$ p

7. *Cost of standard portion* (assume it to be a 7 oz portion)
1 oz costs 0.178 p
7 oz cost 7 × 0.178 = £1.24

FORECASTING

Often the question is asked how restaurants know how much food to prepare. It is done by forecasting. Forecasting is the ability to predict demand. The restaurateur must be able to estimate reasonably accurately what the sales will be. This is important since it avoids waste and prevents shortages. Waste can be avoided through accurate buying and careful production of food. Forecasting the volume of sales of an establishment for a particular period is called production planning or volume forecasting.

Sometimes forecasting is relatively simple as is the case with banquets. The expected number is known in advance of the function and therefore arrangements can be made accordingly. An industrial canteen has a fair idea of expected meals to be prepared because of its knowledge of the number of workers. From experience, a general hospital kitchen will know, for example, that there will be less routine surgery during summer and at Christmas time, and therefore fewer patients, than during say May or October. With this advance knowledge plans can be made accordingly.

Forecasting is more difficult for a commercial establishment particularly if it has a complex menu. The caterer has to predict not only the number of customers but also the dishes that the customers will select from the menu. This problem is minimised in a 'cook to order' establishment such as a steak-house. While it is very rarely possible to be totally accurate, it is, however, necessary to establish a system which will forecast the total consumption of food and drink. New developments like the cook-chill systems and the *sous-vide* method go a long way to assist in minimising losses through unsold cooked food.

To assist with the task of forecasting the caterer must examine the sales histories. These are records showing analysed sales figures. By keeping a daily record of the expected and the actual sales it is possible to make predictions. Through a careful examination of all the available information, the popularity of past menus and dishes can be estimated. This will also indicate the customers' likes and dislikes.

Apart from historical information the restaurateur will need to assess external factors. Dramatic weather changes affect sales. A sudden spell of very hot weather or snowfall may keep people away. Weather also affects the choice of menu. Road closure for repairs can have an adverse effect. Local festivals or celebrations will increase demand. It is therefore by careful analysis that demand can be anticipated and therefore planned.

Once output or sales have been estimated, the correct amount of food can be ordered. Earlier, the importance of the standard recipe was explained. 'Standard recipes' are prepared so that by following its instructions a 'standard yield' may be achieved. Similarly, through strict control of 'standard portions' the right number of people are fed in a fair and satisfactory manner.

PORTION CONTROL

The size of the portion, i.e. the standard portion, is determined by the type of outlet. In a high-class restaurant where price is not the all-important factor, a larger portion is expected than at a more modest establishment where price is the determining factor. Portion control is therefore a routine to serve an amount of food which will satisfy the customer on the one hand, and provide the establishment with a reasonable profit on the other. The simple rule to be guided by would be a fair size at a fair price. Depending on the type of clientele the size of the portion can determine customer satisfaction. For example, too small an amount served in a restaurant catering for either young or well-to-do people may result in the customer feeling cheated. On the other hand, surveys have shown that too large a portion served in an establishment catering for old people may result in loss of sales because the customer may be reluctant to patronise a place where, it is felt, wasted food will be reflected in the price! Weak portion control can also mean loss of revenue to the proprietors. A restaurant serving 1,000 steaks could lose £250 if each steak is 1 oz over the standard portion size.

As already explained the cost per portion of a large number of foods may be determined by dividing the unit cost by the number of portions obtainable from that unit. For example if a melon can produce six slices and the melon costs 72 p the cost of one portion is 12 p (0.72/6). If an egg-tray (30 eggs) cost £1.12 and the standard portion for a particular establishment consists of two poached eggs the cost of that portion would be

$$\frac{1.12}{30} \times 2 = 0.075 \text{ p}$$

To control portions it is necessary to have available:
1. Adequate preparation equipment, e.g. scales, moulds, baking tins.
2. Appropriate serving equipment, e.g. ladles, glasses, vegetable dishes, optics.
3. Staff training; very often caterers have the equipment but staff are not properly trained to appreciate the importance of serving the correct portions.

Many establishments provide visual displays of dishes to assist the staff to familiarise themselves with the required size and presentation of the portions.

Pre-portioned foods are available in increasing numbers. The most common of these are the prepacked packs of milk, jam, butter, sauces and of course tea-bags. However, pre-portioned foods also include items like steaks for steak-bars or chicken drumsticks. Desserts can also be bought prepacked, thus making portion control easier. These pre-wrapped items are easy to cost as they are bought for an agreed price and costed accordingly by the restaurateur. Other advantages apart from cost control are consistency of quality, more hygienic handling, minimum stock levels, reduced labour costs and more choice. An estimated 80 per cent of caterers currently use pre-portioned packs of one form or another.

Whichever system is in use portion control needs not only the co-operation of well-trained staff but also constant supervision by management. Spot checks are a useful way of ensuring that portion control is being carried out effectively.

SUMMARY

1. Wastage of any kind comes under the control of management.
2. Wastage occurs in stages: storage; preparation; cooking; serving.
3. Standard yield is the edible part of food which an establishment expects from particular amounts of food.
4. The aim of portion control is to keep costs to a minimum; maximise profits; give customer satisfaction and avoid waste.
5. Portion control can be assisted through the use of appropriate equipment during preparation and serving; well-trained staff and the purchasing of pre-portioned food.

ASSIGNMENT

1. In which areas of food preparation does wastage mainly occur?
2. How can the percentage loss in fruits and vegetables be affected?
3. Why is profitability affected by the way a meat joint is roasted?
4. What are causes of plate waste?
5. Explain what is meant by yield.
6. Explain forecasting and why it is necessary.
7. List factors affecting forecasting.
8. State aids to efficient portion control.
9. Explain what is meant by portion control.
10. Give two examples of portion-control equipment used in:
    (a)   the kitchen;
    (b)   the restaurant;
    (c)   the bar.
11. How do 'standard recipes' contribute to portion control?
12. Explain how badly trained staff affect the efficient control of portions.
13. For each of the following examples (a)–(f) find:
    A   Waste (%);
    B   Usable weight (%);
    C   Cost of usable weight;

D   Cost of standard portion.

(a) A headed salmon weighing 11 lb 6 oz is purchased at £2.95 per lb. After preparing and cooking it is found to weigh 9 lb 12 oz (6 oz portions are required).

(b) Cooking-apples weighing 20 lb are bought for preparation into apple filling. After peeling and coring the usable weight of the apples is 15 lb. The price was £0.16 per lb (ignore D).

(c) A joint of smoked gammon weighing 14 lb is purchased at 122 p per lb. After cooking and carving it weighed 11 lb 4 oz (portion size required 10 oz).

(d) 22 kg of beef is purchased at £6.00 per kg. After boning, trimming, cooking and carving it is found that 20.76 kg is obtained (4 oz portion required).

(e) 90 lb of veal was delivered to our kitchens at 214 p per lb. After preparation and cooking 67 lb 3 oz was left (the portion size required is 5 oz).

(f) A 56 lb sack of new potatoes cost £2.30. After peeling it is found that 293 × 3 oz portions were served.

14. *Portion calculations:* Estimate the number of portions that can be obtained from the following food products.

Product and weight		Preparation loss	Portion size	No. of portions
Headed salmon	11 lb 1 oz	1 lb 10 oz	4 oz	
Lemon soles	68.040 kg	29.480 kg	6 oz	
Beef	22 kg	13 kg	90 g	
Potatoes	56 lb	2 lb	3 oz	
Smoked gammon	14 lb	2 lb 12 oz	10 oz	
Veal joint	90 lb	23 lb	5 oz	
Roast turkey	21 lb 9 oz	6 lb 2 oz	8 oz	
Chicken	15 lb 10 oz	2 lb 3 oz	360 g	
Leg of lamb	5 lb 5 oz	22.5%	150 g	
Veal escalope	25 kg 44 g	900 g	3 oz	
Lobster	2 lb 10 oz	65%	360 g	
Cod	10 lb 2 oz	24%	125 g	

Note: 1 oz = 28.35 g.

1 kg = 2 lb 3.27 oz
1 kg = 1000 g
1 g = 0.03503

7

GROSS PROFIT

The business of the hotelier or restaurateur is to sell goods and services at a profit. Income from sales must be sufficient to cover his food cost, that is, the cost of the ingredients used. It must also leave some over to cover all expenses of the business and still leave a fair amount which will be an adequate reward for the investment in the business.

The difference between sales (i.e. income), and the cost of food and drink, (i.e. cost of materials used), is known as the **gross profit** (GP). Sometimes it is referred to as **kitchen profit** and if sales relate solely to the bars it is often called **bar profit**. In this text it will be referred to as gross profit.

The first thing that must be remembered is that

Sales − Food cost = Gross profit

EXAMPLE

A cake is sold for £3.25 and the ingredients cost £1.50. The gross profit is therefore £1.75.

Calculation

It was sold for £3.25 (i.e. sales)	3.25
Ingredients cost £1.50 (i.e. food cost)	1.50
Sales − Food cost = Gross profit	1.75

If Sales − Food cost = Gross profit, it follows that

Sales	**− Gross profit**	**= Food cost**
3.25	− 1.75	= 1.50 (Look at the example above)

It must be understood that the total sum of food cost and gross profit is equal to the amount of sales, so that therefore:

Food cost	**+ Gross profit**	**= Sales**
1.50	+ 1.75	= 3.25 (Look at the example ab

Looked at as a cake (Fig. 7.1) would be divided into two parts. Food cost plus gross profit would together form the whole cake, which represents the selling price. In Fig. 7.2 notice that food cost is shown at the £1.50 level. The remainder, up to £3.75, represents the gross profit.

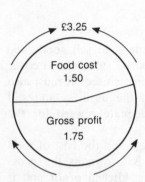

FIG. 7.1 Food cost and gross profit

FIG. 7.2 Food cost and gross profit

Fill in the following. The first one is already worked out.

	Sales (£)	Food cost (£)	Gross profit (£)
(1)	2.50	1.05	1.45
(2)	4.00	2.40	
(3)	3.50		2.30
(4)		2.60	1.30
(5)	16.00	7.50	
(6)	14.50		8.25
(7)		10.50	5.60
(8)	20.00	12.00	
(9)		11.30	8.70
(10)	16.00		9.75

EXERCISES 1

Now try some examples. Check the answers for exercises 1 and 2 given below before continuing. Don't forget to write out the formula each time – it will help you memorise it.

Sales − Food cost = Gross profit

1. The food cost of a dish is £0.80. Find the gross profit if the dish is sold for £1.25.
2. A flan aux cerises was sold for £2.50 and cost £1.75 in ingredients. Find the gross profit.

> *ANSWER 1.*
>
> | Sales | − Food costs | = Gross profit |
> |-------|--------------|----------------|
> | 1.25 | − 0.80 | = 0.45 |
>
> *ANSWER 2.*
>
> | Sales | − Food costs | = Gross profit |
> |-------|--------------|----------------|
> | 2.50 | − 1.75 | = 0.75 |

3. A soufflé Milanaise was sold for £2.75 which gave a gross profit of £1.25. What was the food cost?
4. Chicken and mushroom vol-au-vent cost 48 p to produce. The restaurant wants its gross profit to be 35p. How much should it be sold for?
5. Bacon and eggs and chips sells for £2.25. The cost of the food is £1.50. What is its gross profit?
6. Drinks sold at the bar amounted to £65,250.00 and the cost of materials to £32,160. Find out the gross profit made.
7. The sales amounted to £4,500, the food cost was £2,300. What was the gross profit?
8. The meal at a banquet had material cost of £3,260, the total income was £7,600. What was the gross profit?
9. Find out the gross profit on roast chicken if the food cost was £1.26 and it sold for £2.65.
10. A restaurant used £10,600 for materials and had sales of £32,000 for the same period. What was the gross profit?

We have so far learned that:
(a) 'Sales' means the money taken in from selling food and drink.
(b) Food cost is the total cost of the materials or ingredients used in producing the food for sale.
(c) Gross profit is the difference between what it costs to produce and the selling price. This difference must be sufficient to

cover the running costs of the business and leave over an adequate return for the owner. The gross profit is also sometimes referred to as 'kitchen profit' or 'bar profit'.

The gross profit is expressed as a percentage of sales and the formula used is:

$$\frac{\textbf{Gross profit}}{\textbf{Sales}} \times \frac{\textbf{100}}{\textbf{1}}$$

So that if we look at the first example (page 00) the gross profit was £1.75 and the sales £3.25. Expressed as a percentage this would be

$$\frac{1.75}{3.25} \times \frac{100}{1} = 53.85\%$$

The gross profit percentage is fixed by management as part of its sales policy for the establishment. It is therefore most important for the chef to adhere to the percentage set, as this is representative of the kitchen's contribution to the overall profitability of the establishment. If the gross profit percentage achieved is continuously lower (or indeed higher) than that expected, investigations must be made to determine why. (In later chapters we shall examine reasons for this.)

It must be remembered that the food cost percentage and the gross profit percentage = sales (which is always 100 per cent).

Complete the following chart which gives some examples of gross profit (GP) percentages. The first one should be completed like this:

FC%	GP%	Sales
25	75	100

Food cost %	Gross profit %	Sales	Example
	75		Appetiser
45			Meat dish

Food cost %	Gross profit % Sales	Example
25		Vegetables
	80	Sweet
	45	Draught beer
46		Hamburger
	60	Bottled beer
35		Soft drinks
	70	Spirits
20		Coffee

EXERCISE 2

As you work through the following exercises remember to write out the formula each time before working out the calculations. This will help you memorise the formula.

Do the first one and then check the answer below.

Sales − Food cost   = Gross profit
1.20 − 0.75   = 0.45

$$\frac{\text{Gross profit}}{\text{Sales}} \times \frac{100}{1}$$

$$\frac{0.45}{1.20} \times \frac{100}{1} = 37.5\% = G^p\%$$

1. The food cost of ham and cheese salad is £0.75. Find the gross

profit as a percentage of the selling price if the dish is sold for £1.20.

2. An apple flan was sold for £2.25 and the food cost was £1.60. Find the GP percentage.

3. The takings at Charlie's Bar for one week were £6,400. The cost of the drinks sold was £3,850. Calculate the GP percentage.

4. The selling price of a meal is £11.50 and the gross profit is £4.60. What is the GP percentage?

5. The total cost of drinks sold at the Grotto Bar amounted to £55,440 and sales to £158,585. Find the GP percentage.

6. What were the sales if gross profit was £45,500 and cost of food was £24,500?

7. If the gross profit was £55,550 and the food cost was £25,450, how much were the sales?

8. The price of a set menu is £9.50 and the GP percentage is 65 per cent. Calculate the cost of food.

9. The selling price for a buffet for 65 people was £747.50. The food cost per head was £3.68. Find the GP percentage for this buffet.

10. What was the gross profit if sales were £4,500 and the GP percentage was 63 per cent?

11. The expected weekly GP percentage at Jacko's was 66 per cent. On a particular week takings amounted to £8,350 and the cost of food and drink sold for that week was £3,065. By how much did the actual GP percentage differ from the expected GP percentage?

12. The sales were £33,000 and the food cost percentage was 29 per cent. How much was the gross profit and the cost of food?

13. Steak, mushrooms and tomatoes cost £1.20, £0.20 and £0.15 respectively and the selling price for the dish is £2.75. If the cost of steak goes up by 12 per cent find the new selling price needed to keep the same gross profit.

14. Egg and chips are priced at Marie's at £1.50. On this price her gross profit is £0.70. If the cost of food goes up by 10 per cent find the selling price in order to maintain his £0.70 gross profit.

15. A three-course meal at a restaurant came to £15.75 which included a bottle of wine priced at £3.50. The starter and the dessert totalled £3.75. The food cost for the whole meal, but excluding wine, was £6.25. Find: (a) the selling price of the main course; (b) the gross profit of the food (i.e. excluding the wine).

OPENING AND CLOSING STOCK

We have been using the **food cost** and **sales** as a means of finding the **gross profit**. It was also explained that food cost is the actual cost of the food and drinks used in producing a dish, in other words the cost of the ingredients. If we were making a cake just once, we could carefully buy all the ingredients needed and use them all up in making that one cake. There would be no ingredients left over. However, a catering kitchen could not be run efficiently if the chef had to go out to the supermarket with a shopping list every time a dish was to be produced. It is therefore necessary to hold stocks that may be needed for more than one dish and stocks which may not be used up totally. These items of 'left-over stocks' must be taken into account when calculating the food cost. To calculate the cost of food it is necessary, therefore, to know the value of stock on the shelves. This is called *opening stock*. To this figure is added the cost of the food brought into the kitchen, this is either the direct supplies like perishables or items requisitioned from the dry stores. This is known as *purchases*. The value of any items of stock left over, after producing the food, is deducted. This is called the *closing stock*. The closing stock for one period becomes the opening stock for the following period. For example, the stocks at 1 a.m. when the restaurant shuts are the closing stocks for that day's account. The same figure becomes the opening stocks later in the morning when the business starts functioning again. All this is neatly shown by the formula:

Opening stock + Purchases − Closing stock = Cost of food sold (i.e. Food cost)

EXAMPLE

Le Coq d'Or is a restaurant which begins the day with stocks in the kitchen worth £320 (*opening stock*). During the day goods are bought (*purchases*) to the value of £460. After the food for the day has been prepared £335 worth of stock remains on the kitchen shelves (*closing stock*). Find the food cost.

	£
Opening stock	320
+ Purchases	460
	780
− Closing stock	335
= Food cost	445

Assuming that sales for that day were £986, find the gross profit.

Remember
Sales − Food cost = Gross profit
986   − 445   = 541

To find the gross profit percentage we need

$$\frac{\textbf{Gross profit}}{\textbf{Sales}} \times \frac{\textbf{100}}{\textbf{1}}$$

$$\frac{541}{986} \times \frac{100}{1} = 54.87\%$$

Could you see where all the figures came from?

The following three questions will provide you with some practice. Do them and then check the answer. Do not forget – write out the formula as you go along. It may be more cumbersome but it has its advantages – it will help you remember them!

1. At Le Chamonix the opening stock is £400, purchases £600 and closing stock £350. Find the food cost.
2. A restaurant starts the day with opening stocks worth £165, makes purchases during the day of £360 and has a closing stock of £120. Find the food cost.
3. What would the cost of food be if a restaurant purchases £580 worth of goods, ends up with £260 worth of stocks after having started the day with £150 worth of stocks?

ANSWER 1

	£
Opening stock	400
+ Purchases	600
=	1,000
− Closing stock	350
= Food cost	£650

ANSWER 2

	£
Opening stock	165
+ Purchases	360
=	525
− Closing stock	120
= Food cost	£405

ANSWER 3

	£
Opening stock	150
+ Purchases	580
=	730
− Closing stock	260
= Food cost	£470

Revise this chapter before attempting the following questions. Remember always to write out the formula first before starting the calculations.

ASSIGNMENT

Note: For the purpose of this assignment food cost, cost of food, cost of food sold, material costs, ingredient costs are all different ways of representing the same thing, i.e. *Food cost*.

1. Opening stock is £310, closing stock is £148 and purchases are £200. Find the cost of food.
2. The week begins with stock in the kitchen of £65. During the week purchases amount to £420. After the close of the week the stocks are £72. Calculate the food cost.
3. Stocks on 1 May 1986 were £2,360. Stocks on 31 May 1986 were £1,890. Purchases for the period were £7,820. Find the cost of food.
4. Purchases during May were £750. Stock on 1 May was £120, and on 31 May was £180. What was the cost of food during May?
5. Calculate the cost of food for October if stock on 1 October was £170, on 31 October was £180 and purchases for the month amounted to £900.
6. Calculate the cost of food for July if opening stocks were £225, closing stock £210 and purchases £900.
7. Find the cost of food for a newly opened café if the purchases amounted to £235 and closing stock was £158.
8. Opening stock on 1 June was £205, the purchases for the month amounted to £960 and closing stock was £205. Find the cost of food.
9. On 1 February stock was £250. Purchases amounted to £750. Stock on 28 February was £210. Find food cost.
10. On Monday Luigi has £126 worth of stocks in his kitchen. On Tuesday his purchases come to £178. On Thursday more purchases to the value of £163, and on Friday purchases amount to £46. A quick count on Saturday, before closing for the week, show stocks of £132. What was Luigi's food cost for the week?

8

NET PROFIT

In Chapter 7 it was said that the gross profit should be sufficient to cover all the running costs of the business as well as leaving enough for a reasonable return to the proprietors. This return, or reward, given to the proprietors for investing their money in the business, is known as **net profit**. Therefore, the net profit is what is left over after the food cost and all other expenses have been met.

It will be remembered from the previous chapter that:

Sales − Food cost = Gross profit

so if all other expenses are deducted from the *Gross profit* the difference is the *Net profit*, therefore:

Gross profit − Expenses = Net profit

Expenses are usually broken up between labour costs and overheads. This is done so that it can easily be seen how much of the outgoings is being taken up by the employment of staff and how much by all the other expenses such as rent, electricity, etc. (Chapter 9 deals with expenses in more detail.) The formula above therefore becomes:

Gross profit − (Labour costs + Overheads) = Net profit

To find gross profit in the first place, food cost, which is a cost itself, has to be deducted from the total sales (see Ch. 7). Now we go a step further, and if food cost plus labour costs and overheads are deducted from sales then the net profit is obtained. These three types of costs together are known as the **total costs**, therefore:

Sales − (Food costs + Labour costs + Overheads) = Net profit

This is the same as saying that:

Sales − Total costs = Net profit

All this may appear complicated but it is **not**. It is simply two ways of obtaining the same results. The first way goes in stages by deducting food cost from sales which gives gross profit and then by deducting labour costs and overheads from gross profit obtaining net profit.

By the second method, the total of the three costs is simply deducted from sales to obtain the net profit.

Sales − Food Cost   = Gross profit
Gross profit − Labour costs − Overheads = Net profit

Is the same as saying:

Sales − Total costs = Net profit

(not forgetting, of course, that total costs consist of food cost, labour costs and overheads).

EXAMPLE

If sales are £4,000, Food cost £1,300, Labour costs £1,250, Overheads £750, find the net profit.

Method 1		£	*Method 2*		£
Sales		4,000	Sales		4,000
− Food cost		1,300	− Total cost		3,300
= Gross profit		2,700	= Net profit		700
− Labour costs		1,250			
	=	1,450	Food cost	1,300	
− Overheads		750	+ Labour costs	1,250	
= net profit		£ 700	+ Overheads	750	
			= Total costs	£3,300	

Same answer both ways!

Let us look at another cake (Fig. 8.1) and at the information given. Sales £4,000, Food cost £1,300, Labour costs £1,250, Overheads £750; and Net profit £700.

Displayed on a total costs basis (Fig. 8.2) the cake would appear divided as follows: Sales £4,000; Total costs £3,300 (£1,300 + £1,250 + £750); Net profit £700.

In Chapter 7 it was also explained that the gross profit (GP) percentage was a very useful indicator of the kitchen's or bar's performance. There is, similarly, a need to use the net profit (NP) percentage as another indicator of performance. The ultimate aim

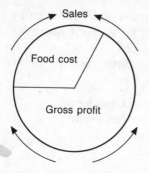

FIG. 8.1 Net profit and expenses

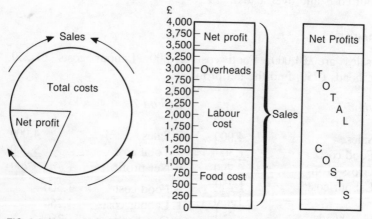

FIG. 8.2 Net profit and total costs

of running a business is to achieve a profit. The reward to the owners must be adequate. The net profit expected must relate to the investment, that is, the amount of money the owners have put into the catering venture. As with gross profit, the net profit percentage is expressed as a percentage of sales and the formula is:

$$\frac{\text{Net profit}}{\text{Sales}} \times \frac{100}{1}$$

The return must, at its very worst, at least equal that which could be obtained by investing the money in any of the financial institutions available. The net profit percentage provides that indication of the relation between the capital invested in the business and the return or gains on that capital. The net profit percentage is a very useful indicator of the final results of any business transaction.

SUMMARY

1. Net profit is the difference between sales and costs.
2. Net profit is the reward to owners for investing in the business.
3. Total costs consist of food cost, labour costs and overheads.
4. Net profit percentage indicates the value of the return on the investment.

ASSIGNMENT

Work out the following examples and check the answers for 1 and 2 before continuing.

1. The students' snack-bar sold food to the value of £4,500. The cost of that food was £1,800. Expenses for the same period amounted to £2,350. Calculate:
   (a)   the gross profit;
   (b)   the net profit;
   (c)   the NP percentage.
2. If sales were £4,000 and the gross profit was £1,500 what was the cost of food?

Answer 1

	£
Sales	4,000
Food cost	1,800
− Gross profit	2,700
− Total costs	2,350
= Net profit	£ 350

$$\frac{\text{Net profit}}{\text{Sales}} \times \frac{100}{1} = \text{NP}\%$$

Therefore $\dfrac{350}{4,500} \times \dfrac{100}{1} = 7.77\%$

or

Answer 2

	£
Sales	4,000
− Food cost	2,500
= Gross profit	£1,500

Sales − Food cost = Gross profit

Sales − Gross profit = Food cost
4,000 − 5,000 = £2,500

3. Joe's Café had a weekly sales of £6,000. The food cost was £2,200, wages came to £560, rent £95 and other expenses £395. Calculate:
   (a)   the GP percentage;
   (b)   the NP percentage.
4. If the sales amounted to £6,000; the GP percentage was 60 per cent and the NP percentage was 15 per cent, find:
   (a)   food cost;
   (b)   total cost;
   (c)   gross profit.

5. If the gross profit is £2,000, labour costs £600 and overheads £700 find the net profit.

6. The net profit of Lucian's Bistro is £600. If labour costs and overheads amounted to £500 what was the gross profit?

7. If sales totalled £120,000, food cost was £65,000, wages £15,000 and expenses £12,000 find
   (a)   gross profit.
   (b)   NP percentage.

8. Sales at the Golden Mermaid were £10,000, gross profit £4,000, labour costs £2,200 and net profit £1,000. Find:
   (a)   the cost of food;
   (b)   overheads.

9. Toby's Bar showed a gross profit of £1,100, the net profit was £300, labour costs were £400 and rent and rates amounted to £300. What did the overheads amount to?

10. If total costs are £6,500 and net profit is £1,200 what are sales?

11. A luncheon for 40 people was priced at £480. Food cost was £3.75 per person; labour costs amounted to £95 and overheads to £98. Find the NP percentage.

12. Gross profit was £5,000, overheads £1,600, food cost £2,000 and net profit £900 find:
    (a)   sales;
    (b)   labour costs.

13. Food cost was £3,500, sales £10,000, labour costs £2,200 and NP percentage was 20 per cent. Find:
    (a)   overheads;
    (b)   net profit.

14. The takings on Friday night at the Spinning Wheel amounted to £3,500. The cost of food came to £1,190, labour costs to £910 and overheads to £770.
    Calculate:
    (a)   the net profit for the night;
    (b)   the net profit as a percentage of sales.

15. Sunny Road Café had costs on a particular day of £1,500 and a loss of £250. Calculate the sales for that day.

9
COSTS

Previously, reference was made to the need for every business to make a profit, or in the case of public institutions, for the need to achieve a surplus or adhere to the financial restrictions imposed on them. In either case there are a number of costs that have to be met in order to run the organisation. These costs are referred to as **elements of cost** and consist of material costs, labour costs and overheads. There are some people who argue that because net profit is a reward to the owners for their investment, in reality this is nothing short of a payment and that therefore as a current expense of the business it ought to be classified as one of the elements of cost. In this book net profit will not be treated as an element of cost. The argument put forward is that net profit is not an expense in itself but a surplus between the sales or total income and the expenses of the business.

ELEMENTS OF COST

MATERIAL COSTS

These refer to the cost of food and drink, and in the hotel and catering industry these would be all items of food, wines, beers and spirits and all types of cigarettes, tobaccos and cigars and confectionery. The cost of food is obtained from the 'purchases' made. 'Purchases' is therefore defined as *all goods bought for resale*. It is important that this is understood. If meat and brandy is bought these will be classified as purchases because at some future date the steak will be cooked and sold in the restaurant and the brandy will probably be sold by tots at the bar. If, on the other hand, a frying-pan or toilet paper is bought these will not be classified as purchases because a hotel uses frying-pans but does not sell them, and similarly it stocks toilet paper as a necessary service but does not sell it as part of its business activities.

LABOUR COSTS

This is the cost of employing staff. It is more than just salaries and wages. Labour costs include *all* expenses related to the employment of staff: staff meals and staff accommodation; pensions; the cost of transport for late-night staff; advertising vacancies; the maintenance and security of uniforms; training costs; holidays; staff sickness. National Insurance (Employers) contributions are also included under this heading. National Insurance (employees) contributions are not a cost to the firm as these are collected from the employees and paid to the Government. Labour costs need constant overseeing as they represent such a large area of expenditure.

There is an important distinction between wages and labour costs. 'Wages' is the remuneration paid to workers for their services to an establishment. Labour costs include all expenses related to the employment of staff of which wages is one.

OVERHEADS

This is the cost of running the business. Rent, rates, water rates, electricity and gas are all expenses necessarily incurred in running the business. Similarly costs like insurance, stationery, printing, advertising, cleaning and repairs. Depreciation is a means of charging the reduction in value of an asset to the profits of the business. A refrigerator bought for £1,500 today cannot be said to be worth the same in a year's time, the difference between the cost price and the current price being depreciation.

Having looked at the elements of cost and their relationship to sales it is now necessary to examine costs under various types of behaviour.

CLASSIFICATION OF COSTS

Costs can be divided into direct costs and indirect costs. **Direct costs** are those costs which are *directly connected* with the activity incurring these costs, e.g. the food cost is a direct cost of the kitchen, gas consumed by the ovens would also be a direct cost of the kitchen. However, part of the cost of heating the whole building would be an **indirect cost** of the kitchen. The same principle would apply with labour costs. The chef's wages would be a direct cost of the kitchen whereas the salary of the food and beverage manager would be an indirect cost to the kitchen.

Indirect costs are therefore those costs which cannot wholly be allocated to a department.

COST BEHAVIOUR

Costs are also labelled according to the way in which they behave. There are costs that move 'in sympathy', i.e. they tend to move with sales. Food costs move in proportion to sales. As sales go up so more food has to be bought to meet that demand. This type of cost is known as **variable cost**. The example below details this kind of cost and is illustrated in graph form in Fig. 9.1.

EXAMPLE

Variable costs: An apple costs 10p (food cost) and sells for 15p. Every time an extra apple is sold the sales go up but the food cost also goes up.

Apples sold	Food costs (p)	Sales (p)
1	10	15
2	20	30
3	30	45
4	40	60
5	50	75

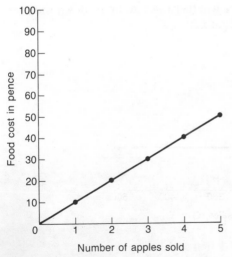

FIG. 9.1 Variable Costs

It will be seen that as the sales go up so does the food cost, i.e. the variable cost.

Fixed costs remain static despite movements in sales. A good example is rent. The rent of a restaurant would remain the same whether the restaurant was fully booked or whether only two people were dining. It would make no difference as the same amount of rent would have to be paid in either case. A fixed-cost example is given below and as a graph in Fig. 9.2.

EXAMPLE

Fixed costs: Say that the rent of the restuarant was £20 per day.

Sales (£)	Rent (£)
100	20
200	20
300	20
500	20
50	20
Restaurant closed	
0	20

It will be seen that no matter whether sales go up or down the rent remains the same, i.e., fixed, at £20.

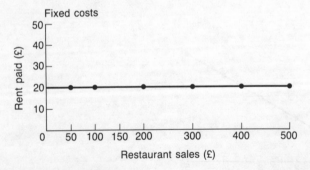

FIG. 9.2 Fixed Costs

There are many costs which are variable in nature but which do not move in the same proportion as the movements in sales. These are **semi-variable costs**. An example would be the consumption of electricity which would move upwards or downwards depending on how many meals are being prepared on an electric cooker. It would move, like variable costs, in sympathy with movements in sales. However, unlike variable costs it would not move at the same rate as the movements in sales.

There are yet other costs that are both variable and fixed by nature. A good example of this would be demonstrated in a gas bill. The standard charge is fixed but the gas charges are variable. This means that whether or not any gas is used the standard charge is there, but the amount of the bill relating to the use of gas depends on the actual consumption of gas. This type of cost is also known as semi-variable costs. (Semi-variable costs are sometimes referred to as semi-fixed costs.)

EXAMPLE

Assume British Gas charges 20p per therm and £10 standing charge

Therms	With no Standing charge	With £10 Standing charge
0	£ 0	£ 0 + £10 = £ 10
100	£ 20	£ 20 + £10 = £ 30
200	£ 40	£ 40 + £10 = £ 50
300	£ 60	£ 60 + £10 = £ 70
400	£ 80	£ 80 + £10 = £ 90
500	£100	£100 + £10 = £110

Compare the following two graphs (Figs. 9.3 and 9.4) for the consumption of gas. Figure 9.3 shows the consumption of gas without any standing charge (variable cost). Figure 9.4 shows the same consumption but with the addition of the standing charge (semi-variable cost).

When comparing both graphs notice that the variable cost curve starts at 0 when no therms are used, whereas the semi-variable cost curve starts at £10 regardless of whether any therms have been used.

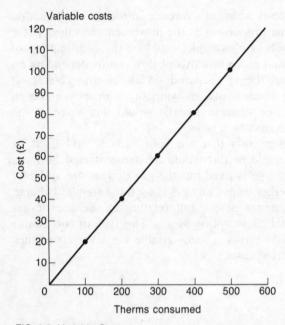

FIG. 9.3 Variable Costs

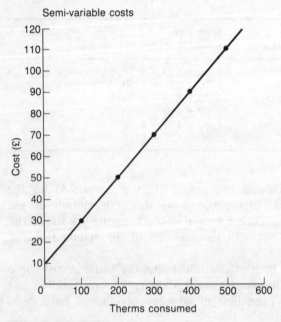

FIG. 9.4 Semi-variable costs

SUMMARY

1. The elements of cost are: materials; labour; overheads.
2. Direct costs are cost directly connected with the activity incurring those costs.
3. Indirect costs are only partly related to the activity.
4. Cost can be classified in accordance with movement as:
   (a) *fixed costs* – remain the same regardless of movements in sales;
   (b) *variable costs* – move in proportion to movements in sales;
   (c) *semi-variable* (semi-fixed) costs – move partly with movements in sales but not in proportion. They are also sometimes partly fixed and partly variable.
5. Wages and labour costs are distinct, wages being an item of labour costs.

ASSIGNMENT

1. Name the elements of cost.
2. Define 'purchases'.
3. What is the difference between wages and labour costs?
4. Explain the difference between direct and indirect costs.
5. Give an example of a variable cost.
6. Explain what a semi-variable is.
7. What is depreciation?
8. List six items which are classified as overheads.
9. Name five items of labour cost.
10. Explain how costs affect net profit.

SELLING PRICE

It should have become clear by now that when fixing a selling price it must be set at a level which is sufficient to cover:

1. Food cost (cost of materials used);
2. Labour costs (cost of employing people);
3. Overheads (cost of all other expenses necessary to run the business);
4. Net profit (reward to owner(s) for investing in the business).

It is quite reasonable to assume that the higher the price charged the greater will be the profit. However, in practice this is not always so as price fixing is a complex matter. The caterer is influenced by a number of internal and external factors that determine the price that may be charged.

INTERNAL FACTORS

1. *Type of customer*. This is the clientele for which the establishment seeks to cater. The variety of menu items, portion sizes and consequently the price charged depends on whether the customers are young or old, families or business people, manual workers or office personnel.
2. *Spending power*. The average spending power (ASP) of the customer affects the quality of food, the standard of service and the portion size. At a high-quality restaurant the ASP could be from £15 to £30 per head while at a more modest steak-house it will be about £10. The effect of price increases varies with the ASP, e.g. a 5p increase in the price of a cup of coffee will be more noticeable and cause more reaction in a small roadside café than a £1 increase in the price of lobster in a luxury restaurant.
3. *Menu*. The type of menu and the time and day of the week when it is available can affect the price charged. A dinner dance on a Saturday will attract a higher price than on a Monday. The

various outlets within an establishment can aim at a different gross profit margin and therefore charge different prices for equivalent dishes. Different gross profit margins can also be applied to an à la carte and a table d'hôte menu.

EXTERNAL FACTORS

1. *Demand.* Customer preference for a particular type of outlet will affect demand which can have an effect on prices charged. For example, an ethnic or speciality restaurant greatly in demand, has more flexibility in its pricing policy.
2. *Competition.* The intensity of competition will have an effect on prices. Generally, the keener the competition the more conscious caterers must be of their prices. It would be appropriate here to mention that many caterers go bankrupt trying to compete by reducing prices without attempting to control their costs – the result being that their costs exceed income and this leads to disaster. The effect of competition on prices is more pronounced among those establishments for which customers have no strong preference. For example, an increase in the price of hamburgers by McDonald's may mean customers switching to Burger King. An increase in the price of hamburgers generally may lead to customers switching from hamburgers to pizzas or fried chicken. The more popular (homogeneous – the correct term) a product is, the more sensitive it is to price variation.
3. *Locality.* Locality will affect pricing strategies. An establishment in the midst of an area containing a large number of low-price outlets must be conscious of competitors' prices. A speciality restàurant in a secluded area whose customers come from far and wide is less likely to be very concerned with competition in other parts. A seasonal establishment may charge higher prices during May to September and lower ones out of season. Similarly, a city restaurant largely patronised by office workers may have different pricing strategies for lunch on Mondays to Fridays to those for dinner on weekday evenings and for weekend business.

The fixing of prices is therefore a management decision. Too low a price may lead to losses and too high a price may lead to bankruptcy arising from lack of customers. When an establishment has been operating for some time there is enough information available from previous years to assist in setting prices. When an establishment is newly opened the pricing policy must be determined by analysing the above factors very carefully. This is an issue that many inexperienced new caterers overlook and suffer the consequences later when they are forced to close down. In fact many small establishments rely on a large element of intuition as well as ingenuity and planning in setting prices acceptable to their clientele.

In most industrial concerns outside catering the actual profit is determined as a percentage of the cost price, that is, it is the 'mark-up'. For example, the total cost of a machine when purchased is £200. The supplier sells it at a price which makes a 10 per cent profit. Therefore the profit is 10 per cent of £200 = £20. The selling price is therefore:

£200 + £20 = **£220**

In the catering industry the method of pricing is through the traditional system of 'profit margin'. The profit is calculated as a percentage of the selling price of the commodity.

When arriving at a pricing policy the caterer must decide what gross profit percentage will be required to cover all the costs as well as the return on the investment (the **net profit**). Thus pricing levels must be based on the total costs of the establishment and determined from experience and previous selling patterns.

To calculate the selling price, therefore, one needs to know the food cost and the gross profit or gross profit percentage. This percentage will have been decided by management after calculating all costs to be covered.

It was said earlier on that the selling price is always represented by 100 per cent. It will also be remembered that:

Selling price − Food cost = Gross profit

similarly:

Selling price (100%) − Food cost % = Gross profit %

or

Selling price (100%) − Gross profit % = Food cost %

With the use of the following formula the selling price can be calculated:

$$\frac{\text{Food cost}}{\text{Food cost \%}} \times \frac{100}{1} = \textbf{Selling price}$$

The food cost (FC) can be obtained from the dish-costing cards.

The food cost percentage is acquired by deducting the agreed gross profit percentage from 100 (100 − GP% = FC%). Different menu items have different gross profit percentage.

EXAMPLE

Steak and mushroom pie costs 50p. Find the selling price to give a gross profit percentage of 60 per cent.

$$\frac{\text{Food cost}}{\text{Food cost \%}} \times \frac{100}{1} = \text{Selling price}$$

$$\frac{0.50}{40} \times \frac{100}{1} \qquad = \text{£1.25}$$

(Remember that 100 − GP% = FC% so in the above 100 − 60 = 40.)

Work through the following examples remembering always to use the formula

$$\frac{\text{Food cost}}{\text{Food cost\%}} \times \frac{100}{1}$$

before calculating the answer.

1. Find the selling price of soused herring if the cost price is 85 p and the GP percentage required is 45 per cent.
2. Chou-fleur à la Grecque costs 42 p. What would be the selling price if you require a 60 per cent gross profit?
3. A portion of dressed crab costs £1.25 to produce. If you are seeking a gross profit of 55 per cent what should you sell it at?
4. What would you have to sell Chicken Maryland at if you want a gross profit of 65 per cent and it costs you £1.30 to make?
5. A portion of ravioli costs 22 p to prepare. Find the selling price if you are seeking a gross profit of 75 per cent.
6. Convenience soup at £8 per tin serves 200 × $\frac{1}{2}$ pint portions, calculate the selling price per portion to give a 95 per cent gross profit.
7. A tub of Westcol ready-to-serve potato salad costs £5.56 and serves 50 × $2\frac{1}{2}$ oz portions. Calculate the selling price per portion if you are seeking a 45 per cent gross profit.
8. Sole goujons cost 68 p per portion to prepare. Find the selling price per portion if you wish to make a gross profit of 55 per cent.
9. 250 portions of ready-to-serve coleslaw cost £7.75. Find the selling price per portion if you are seeking a 45 per cent gross profit.

10. Truite amande cost £1.13 to produce. If you wish to make a 60 per cent gross profit what should the selling price be?
11. Complete the following chart.

Dish	Food cost p	FC%	GP%	Selling price
Leek and potato soup	10.192	25		
Steak and kidney pie	33.923		65	
Marquise potatoes	5.269		80	
Buttered carrots	8.726	30		
Apple pie	11.405		50	
Fresh custard	7.865	25		

12. Compare the selling price of the following dishes under the different percentages.

Dish	Food cost(£)	30% GP	40% GP	50% GP	60% GP
Canard à l'orange	2.756				
Crème caramel	0.158				
Bread and butter pudding	0.226				
Navarin of lamb	0.241				
Watercress soup	0.207				

13. The list below shows the estimated food cost for the named dishes. Next to it the selling price for two competing restaurants are shown. Calculate the gross profit which both restaurants are making for each dish. The first one (rump steak) is worked out below.*

Dish	Same for both restaurants Estimated food cost	Restaurant A Selling price (£)	GP%	Restaurant B Selling price (£)	GP%
Rump steak	2.581	7.35	65	8.00	68
Escalope holstein	1.805	5.65		5.15	
Pomme purée	0.231	0.90		0.85	
Mushroom soup	0.363	0.95		1.10	
Plaice veronique	0.956	2.70		3.00	
Pasta	0.211	0.60		0.65	
Poached haddock	0.723	2.90		2.60	

*Restaurant A:

$$\frac{\text{Food cost}}{\text{selling price}} \times \frac{100}{1} = \frac{2.581}{7.35} \times \frac{100}{1} = 35\% \text{ FC}\%$$

Therefore
100 − 35 = 65%
GP%   = **65%**

*Restaurant B:

$$\frac{\text{Food cost}}{\text{selling price}} \times \frac{100}{1} = \frac{2.581}{8.00} \times \frac{100}{1} = 32\% \text{ FC}\%$$

Therefore
100 − 32 = 68%
GP%   = **68%**

VAT AND SERVICE CHARGE

In April 1973 the Government introduced value added tax (VAT). Basically this is a form of purchase tax in that every time a sale of certain commodities is made a levy is charged at every stage the commodities pass hands or ownership. The current rate is 15 per cent. This means that when the selling price has been calculated a 15 per cent charge must be added to the price. This extra is not 'profit' for the establishment but a tax which the establishment has to collect on behalf of the Government from the customer and send to Customs and Excise.

EXAMPLE

The food cost for fresh prawn salad is £1.20. Find the selling price including VAT to give a gross profit of 55 per cent.

$$\frac{\text{Food cost}}{\text{Food cost \%}} \times \frac{100}{1} = \text{Selling price}$$

$$\frac{1.20}{45} \times \frac{100}{1} \qquad = £2.67$$

Add 15% VAT

$$\frac{15}{100} \times \frac{2.67}{1} \qquad = £0.40$$

$$0.40 + 2.67 \qquad = £3.07$$

Price at which salad must be sold **£3.07**

Many establishments add a service charge to the price of the meal. The service charge must be calculated before VAT is added (because service is subject to VAT). If, for example, in the above calculation a 10 per cent service charge were to be added to the selling price the salad would then sell for £3.38, calculated as follows:

$$\frac{\text{Food cost}}{\text{Food cost \%}} \times \frac{100}{1} = \text{Selling price}$$

$$\frac{1.20}{45} \times \frac{100}{1} \qquad = £2.67$$

Add 10% service charge:

$$\frac{10}{100} \times \frac{2.66}{1} \qquad = £0.27$$

$$2.67 + 0.27 \qquad = £2.94$$

Add 15% VAT

$$\frac{15}{100} \times \frac{2.94}{1} \qquad = £0.44$$

$$2.94 + 0.44 \qquad = \textbf{£3.38}$$

A common error when calculating service charge and VAT is to add both percentages and multiply by the selling price. This of course gives the wrong answer!

ASSIGNMENT

1. The food cost for a banquet is calculated at £3.50 per head. Find the selling price including $12\frac{1}{2}$ per cent service charge and 15 per cent VAT if a 55 per cent gross profit is sought.
2. Find the selling price inclusive of 15 per cent VAT of the following dishes to provide a gross profit of 70 per cent:
   (a)   Cheese salad food cost £0.456;
   (b)   Ham salad food cost £0.568;
   (c)   Prawn salad food cost £1.75;
   (d)   Crab salad food cost £1.20.
3. Find the selling price for a meal costing £4.00 to produce a gross profit of 65 per cent. The price must show a $12\frac{1}{2}$ per cent service charge and 15 per cent VAT.
4. Four neighbouring hotels offer set teas. The food cost for the four hotels is the same, that is, £1.25. Find the selling price for each of the hotels if:
   Hotel A seeks 65% GP;
   Hotel B 74% GP;
   Hotel C 80% GP;
   Hotel D 54% GP.
   Each hotel adds $12\frac{1}{2}$ per cent service charge and 15 per cent VAT.
5. The food cost of Poulet Sauté Parmentier comes to £1.7143; calculate the selling price at the following GP percentage: 55%; 60%; 62%; 65%; 68%; to include 15 per cent VAT.
6. The food cost of fried fillet of plaice is £0.935. Calculate the selling price to produce a GP percentage of: 56%; 69%; 72%; plus 15 per cent VAT.
7. Calculate each of the following dishes to produce different selling prices at GP percentage of: 50%; 57%; 62%; 68%; 73%. Each selling price must include 15 per cent VAT.
   (a) Crème Crecy food cost £0.176
   (b) Crème St Germain food cost £0.182
   (c) Kebab à la turque food cost £0.896
   (d) Poulet sauté food cost £0.587
   (e) Celeri braise food cost £0.197
   (f) Sole colbert food cost £1.098
   (g) Poisson bretonne food cost £1.322
   (h) Ragoût de bœuf food cost £0.978
   (i) Omelette fromage food cost £0.364
   (j) Lemon curd tart food cost £0.263

11

BUDGETARY CONTROL

From a very early age in life everyone is involved in budgeting. The young child saving to buy a toy from weekly pocket money is performing a form of budgeting. Some money can be spent on sweets and some must be put away to buy the desired toy. At a later stage in life budgeting becomes more complicated and more serious. From one's wages, arrangements must be made to pay the immediate and unavoidable expenses like rent, food and transport as well as saving for holidays, and probably paying for an insurance policy or pension scheme. In other words, in both cases a planning of finance takes place. They both have a plan for the future. This plan is in monetary terms. In the case of the worker there are two types of plan. A short-term one budgeting for day-to-day living and holidays, and a long-term one budgeting for the more distant future in the form of an insurance policy.

In business a similar plan is called a budget. A budget is a detailed plan which provides the means of regulating the progress of the business. Budgeting has two roles. One is **planning**, that is, setting out in realistic terms what the business is going to do. The aim of this planning exercise is to achieve the targets which are set. The second role of budgeting is that of **monitoring**. This ensures that the specific tasks are carried out and that targets set are achieved. If the targets are not achieved then the reason why must be determined.

It is a mistake to believe that a budgetary system is for big organisations only. Budgets are as necessary for small businesses as they are for large ones. It is possible that a small business may just have a simple budget mainly concerned with sales. A large organisation has a complex budget with procedures written down in a Budget Manual.

A budget assists management with its forward planning. Management can be either a sole trader running a small restaurant or the board of directors of a large organisation. It will assist in forecasting sales, in estimating production and identifying the resources required to meet the sales targets. A budget expresses the real aspirations of management which can be later compared with the actual results achieved. Budgets should not only be concerned with forecasting sales and costs but also with the control of costs.

In a larger organisation budgetary control is entrusted to a committee consisting probably of the general manager, all heads of departments and the chief accountant. The role of the committee would be to devise a suitable system of budgetary control for their particular organisation. It would define the authority and the responsibility of each head of department in relation to the general objectives of the establishment.

Each department will prepare its own budget. A budget is prepared by estimating the level of expenditure based on previous records for the corresponding period of the year. Variations found in previous periods must be studied and taken into account in the current calculations. An area that may require special attention is labour cost. Any expected wage increase, any reduction or increase in personnel must be accounted for. Market trends need careful consideration; for example, consumer demand for a particular type of food, any changes in consumer spending, how competition is going to affect the operation. Internal changes such as changing the style of service or altering the standard portion sizes or major building expansion work will affect the budget. Uncontrollable external factors like increases in fuel and food prices must be allowed for along with general economic conditions of the nation and in the immediate geographical area in particular.

All the departmental budgets, often referred to as subsidiary budgets, are consolidated into one master budget. The master budget therefore consolidates all expected incomes and expenditure, all assets and liabilities of the organisation.

Budgeting has a salutary effect on individual managers since their involvement in the budget process motivates them into achieving their objectives and keeps them fully informed. As it co-ordinates all aspects of the business, managers become more aware of each other's difficulties, pushing them to work more as a team. Detailed planning focuses on present weaknesses, such as unplanned spending, lack of resources or waste of available resources. The budget sets a standard against which actual performance is measured. It creates a more efficient and responsive accounting system which can produce periodic progress reports for managers.

Budgets are divided into operating and capital budgets. An operating budget is most important. It is a forecast of sales activity and the estimated costs involved in generating those sales. Capital budgets are prepared to deal with the assets and capital items of the business. Capital equipment is typically very costly and plans must be made to provide the necessary finance to purchase or replace it.

Budgets are further subdivided into fixed and flexible. Fixed budgets have fixed amounts allocated for expenditure before the commencement of the budget period. For example, advertising and office expenses are each allotted a fixed sum and expenditure on these items must be kept within the limits of the budget set. These are independent of the level of turnover. Flexible budgets (also referred to as variable budgets) have the expenditure predetermined as a proportion of the level of sales and must therefore be affected by movements in the level of turnover.

It is necessary to distinguish clearly between 'budget' and 'budgetary control'. A budget is a carefully estimated forecast of future financial transactions, i.e. a forecast of income and spending levels. The preparation of the budget will enable future plans to be foreseen, decided upon and implemented. Budgetary control enables actual performance to be compared with budget figures. It is concerned with the investigation of variances (differences) which enables management to enquire into malpractices and instigate corrective action.

Budgets are not only useful to commercial enterprises. They are also extremely important in the industrial and welfare sector. In the National Health Service, for example, a catering manager will be allocated a specific amount of finance worked out on a per capita (per patient) basis. The catering manager has to run the catering department within those figures. Similarly, an industrial caterer must keep within the budget imposed by the subsidy agreed by management. The aim is to break even.

SUMMARY

1. The roles of budgeting are: (a) planning; (b) monitoring.
2. Budgets are as necessary for small businesses as for large organisations.
3. Budgeting is a control tool for management.
4. A subsidiary budget is a departmental one, a master budget is a consolidation of subsidiary budgets.
5. Budgets can be divided into operating budgets and capital budgets.

6. A budget is a plan for future expectations while budgetary control is overseeing the budget.

ASSIGNMENT

1. What are the two main roles of a budget?
2. Explain how a budget can assist management.
3. What is the role of a budget committee?
4. List five factors that need to be considered when preparing a budget.
5. Explain what a master budget is.
6. How can budgets be beneficial to departmental managers?
7. Explain the difference between operating and capital budgets.
8. Explain how fixed and flexible budgets differ.
9. How do budgets and budgetary control differ?
10. How are budgets useful to a non-commercial operation?

12

WINES AND SPIRITS

Beverages can be classified as alcoholic and non-alcoholic. The alcoholic can be subdivided into beers, wines and spirits, and the non-alcoholic into carbonated and non-carbonated (see Fig. 12.1). Carbonated beverages are those drinks such as soda and ginger ale, better known as mixers. The non-carbonated can further be subdivided into items from the still-room, like tea, coffee, milk or the dispense-bar variety of vegetable and fruit juices. In this chapter we shall .refer to beverages as those drinks normally dispensed at a bar and we shall refer to all the other bar items, e.g. olives, nuts, lemons, as bar ingredients.

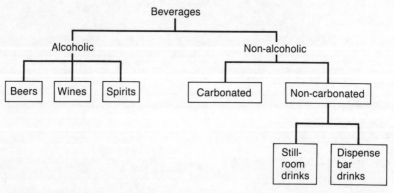

FIG. 12.1 Beverage classification

PURCHASING

Beverage purchasing control is no different from food purchasing control, the main aim being to obtain adequate supplies of acceptable quality at the best price. Standard purchasing specifications and standard purchasing procedures are the key factors. Standard purchasing specifications are easier than those for food because beverages are of a standard size and brand. The purchasing ought to be undertaken by someone well qualified in beverages. When purchasing beverages, particularly wines, care must be taken to ensure that they are suitable for the type of customer being catered for.

BEVERAGES: SOURCES OF SUPPLY

System	Suitability	Advantages	Disadvantages
Wine shippers	(a) Prestigious outlets; (b) Very large companies	Prices lower; high quality; specialised knowledge.	Limited choice; large quantities only; delivery limited.
Wholesaler	Medium/small outlets	Wide range; regular delivery; after-sales service; good promotional material; credit facilities	Prices may be uncompetitive; will 'push' own brand; lack specialised knowledge
Cash & carry	(a) Small establishments; (b) Industrial catering with limited demand	Keen prices; good for emergencies; low outlay	Limited range; no service; no credit
Auctions	(a) Prestigious outlets; (b) Very large companies	Unusual brands; Good prices	Small amounts; not suitable for wine lists
Manufacturers	Very large organisations	Competitive prices	Costs of storage; capital tied up

RECEIVING

Beverages are usually received by the cellarman who has the necessary expertise to check goods for quality. When checking quantities, care must be taken that the right sizes are being delivered and that empty bottles are not included in the crates.

The value of alcoholic beverages is high and therefore careful and methodical checking of goods is very important.

The cellarman will also record all deliveries. This reduces security risks caused when transferring expensive wines and spirits from the receiving area to the cellar area. The ideal time for delivery of beverages is in the afternoon when the receiving bay is less busy. However, suppliers are not always able to do this. Any shortages or wrong deliveries must be noted and a request for credit issued.

STORING

Cellars should ideally be situated, as conveniently as possible, between the receiving bay and the dispensing areas. Every dispensing outlet should maintain sufficient stocks to meet known demand. As the drinks are sold they are replenished from the cellar. This system makes requisition easy and establishes tight control over stocks.

The ideal cellar layout would consist of four areas at differently controlled temperatures. One area is for white and sparkling wines, another for red wines and spirits, another one for beers and a separate area for empties. Most cellars, however, do not have this ideal layout and consequently only have two different temperature-controlled areas, one for white and sparkling wines and another for the rest of the stock. Smaller cellars may have refrigerated space for white and sparkling wines which must be kept at 10 °C (50 °F). Red wines, spirits, beers and soft drinks are kept at 13 °C (55 °F).

Empties are normally kept in a secured caged space near the receiving bay. Care must be taken with empties of beers and soft drinks as these are valuable because deposits have been paid on them. Returnable empties must be counted when returned to suppliers and a credit note sought.

Particular and extra care must be taken with empties of wines and spirits when the establishment operates a 'full for empty' system. Under this system the bar will return to the cellar its empty bottles for replacement by full ones to bring the stock level at the bar back to normal. While this practice ought to be discouraged, there are still many establishments operating under this system. This enables dishonest staff to obtain full bottles for their own use or for dishonestly selling at the bar. As with dry stores, the storage facilities of cellars are dictated to a large extent by the size and the layout of the premises. However, underestimating cellar requirements will create problems of having to find adequate and secure extra space.

Most cellars will have a Cellar Control Book which lists all movements of beverages in and out of the cellar. Depending on its design it can provide information on the level and value of stocks. Every kind of beverage in the cellar will have its bin card similar to that used for food items. The bin card number is the same number as that which will appear in the wine list presented to customers in the restaurant.

Issues are made only on presentation of an authorised requisition form (see Exhibit 12.1). Requisition forms for beverages are normally of a different colour from that for food. In many organisations the colour of the requisition form varies for every department. This eases allocation of departmental costs. Issues are usually costed with two prices. On the one column the 'cost price' is shown and this is used later by the accounts and control office. On another column the issue is costed with the 'selling price' (i.e. the retail price). This is used by the dispensing outlet to calculate and verify its takings by valuing stocks at the bars on a selling-price basis. The total value of beverages consumed must equal the

			DUKES HOTEL 11905		
			WINE AND LIQUOR REQUISITION		
Department			Date		
Bin No.	Units Req	Size	Description	Units Issued	Stock Code

Requisitioned by ....

Issued by ....

Received by ....

EXHIBIT 12.1 Wine and liquer requisition

total amount of revenue received.

Whenever goods are sent from one department to another, e.g. brandy from bar to kitchen or lemons from kitchen to bar, a Transfer Note must be completed so that a written record of movements of items is held. This is also necessary for accounts purposes.

Ullages – substandard or unusable beverages – as well as all breakages must be reported so that the food and beverage controller can keep a record. In large organisations special books are kept for this purpose.

Stock-taking must take place periodically so that the value of stock can be determined and any differences between the actual physical stock and the book stock can be identified. Both excesses and shortages must be investigated. Regular stock-taking also identifies slow-moving items.

It has already been mentioned that beverages being a high-cost item is subject to many tricks in attempts to steal from the establishment. Regular spot checks on stocks in cellars and in bars are necessary. These checks are necessary not just for quantity but to prevent 'adulteration', e.g. by watering, which is illegal, or by substitution.

For security reasons it is essential that references for staff employed in cellars are carefully checked. The cellar should have opening hours and issues outside these times should be discouraged.

COSTING AND SELLING

The preparation of beverages is obviously much easier than the preparation of food. Exquisite preparation is the main factor for food sales, whereas with beverages it is the presentation, such as showmanship in cocktails and careful attention to service, that will increase sales.

Earlier (Ch. 11) the importance of and need for forecasting, i.e. anticipating the volume of sales, was stressed. Forecasting the sale of beverages for each outlet or function is as necessary as forecasting food sales even though, unlike food, beverages are usually non-perishable and therefore little waste occurs. Again as with food, sales histories – in other words keeping detailed records of sales – are very useful in anticipating demand and assisting with purchasing.

Standard yields and its relation to portion control was previously explained when applied to food. Similarly, with beverages every bottle is expected to render a certain yield from which standard portions or standard drink sizes can be calculated and costed accordingly. Portion control is as essential with beverages as with food and therefore either optics or other similar bar dispensing equipment, e.g. standard glassware, must be used. Portion control is also considerably aided by use of standard units, e.g. beer bottles or mixers. Bars with a large and quick turnover may use automatic beverage-dispensing machines. Apart from the strict portion control because of its pre-set drink size, it prevents bar staff from handling bottles. All drinks are obtained by pressing the correct computerised button which dispenses the drink, displays the price, issues the bill and records the transactions for revenue and stock purposes.

Just as standard recipes are prepared for accurate food costing, similarly, they ought to be prepared for beverages as well. It would probably be impractical to write standard recipes for all drink combinations available, but certainly the more popular cocktails served by the outlet should be standardised.

The pricing of beverages can be as complex as the pricing of food. It depends not only on internal factors such as management policy and type of establishment but it is also governed by external ones such as, for example, competition. In commercial catering the caterer will try to maximise profits, but ultimately it is the customers who will decide the price for the type of service being offered. Many establishments still go for the traditional system of adding a percentage profit margin to cost. In pubs, for example, the following GP percentages are generally used: Draught beer 40–45%; Bottled beer 42–50%; Wines and spirits 55–65%; Soft drinks and mixers 50–65%. When costing wines in a restaurant caterers have the predicament that an 'across the board' GP percentage margin may make the price of average wines acceptable but the price of expensive wines prohibitive thus limiting its sale. To deal with this problem a sliding scale of GP percentage margin is used, with the cheaper wines having a larger percentage mark-up than the more expensive wines. Another method in use is to add a cash margin to all wines regardless of cost. This of course makes better-quality wines, as far as the customer is concerned, excellent value for money.

Beverages are purchased either as selling units, e.g. mixers and bottled beers or as whole units to be broken down, e.g. a keg of beer or a bottle of whisky. As some major examining boards still prefer to cost food and drink on a GP percentage basis the following calculations will be based on this system. The equation to use is as that used for food earlier except that 'beverage' substitutes 'food', thus:

$$\text{Selling price} = \frac{\text{Beverage cost}}{\text{Beverage cost \%}} \times \frac{100}{1}$$

EXAMPLE 1

A bottle of Cabernet Sauvignon costing £6.35 must be sold for £16.25 if the restaurateur is seeking 55 per cent GP percentage.

$$\text{Selling price} = \frac{\text{Beverage cost}}{\text{Beverage cost \%}} \times \frac{100}{1}$$

$$\frac{6.35}{45} \times \frac{100}{1} = £14.11$$

(Remember that the beverage cost percentage is the difference between 100 and the GP percentage. In the above example it is (100 − GP%) which is 100 − 55 = 45.)

To this VAT at 15 per cent would need to be added, so that:

$$\frac{15}{100} \times \frac{14.11}{1} = 2.12$$

therefore 14.11 + 2.12 = **£16.23** (say £16.25).

EXAMPLE 2

A similar calculation is required to find the price of, for example, a bottle of beer if the crate of 24 costs £8.56 and the publican is seeking a gross profit of 42 per cent.

Cost of crate is £8.56, therefore, the cost of a bottle is 8.56/24 = 0.36 p.

$$\frac{\text{Beverage cost}}{\text{Beverage cost \%}} \times \frac{100}{1} = \text{Selling price}$$

$$\frac{0.36}{58} \times \frac{100}{1} = 0.62$$

Add VAT at 15 per cent:

$$\frac{15}{100} \times \frac{0.62}{1} = 0.09$$

$$0.62 + 0.09 = 0.71 \text{ p}$$

EXAMPLE 3

Another example is that of one keg of beer costing £42.90. If the publican seeks 40 per cent gross profit, the selling price of a pint is found as follows.

A keg contains 10 gallons and there are 8 pints to the gallon, therefore, there are 80 pints in a keg. The cost of a pint is then:

$$\frac{42.90}{80} = 0.54 \text{ p}$$

$$\frac{\text{Beverage cost}}{\text{Beverage cost \%}} \times \frac{100}{1} = \text{Selling price}$$

$$\frac{0.54}{60} \times \frac{100}{1} = 0.90$$

Add VAT at 15 per cent:

$$\frac{15}{100} \times \frac{0.90}{1} = 0.14$$

Price per pint is 0.90 + 0.14 = **£1.04**

EXAMPLE 4

A bar seeks a GP percentage of 55 per cent on whisky. If a standard bottle yielding 32 measures costs £7.40 find the selling price of a measure. Cost of measure:

$$\frac{7.40}{32} = 0.23 \text{ p}$$

$$\frac{\text{Beverage cost}}{\text{Beverage cost \%}} \times \frac{100}{1} = \text{Selling price}$$

$$\frac{0.23}{45} \times \frac{100}{1} = 0.51 \text{ p}$$

Add VAT at 15 per cent:

$$\frac{15}{100} \times 0.51 = 0.08 \text{ p}$$

Selling price of measure is 0.51 + 0.08 = **0.59 p** (say 0.60 p).

COCKTAILS

To price a cocktail every ingredient must first be costed individually. The total cost of all ingredients is the beverage cost. As with all other costings, from the GP percentages required the selling price will be found to which 15 per cent VAT must be added.

EXAMPLE

Find the selling price of a Rusty Nail with a GP percentage of 55 per cent.

A Rusty Nail consists of: $\frac{1}{6}$ gill Drambuie; $\frac{1}{3}$ gill Scotch whisky. Drambuie costs £10.33 per bottle and whisky £7.40 per bottle. The cost of a tot would be:

$$\text{Drambuie } \frac{10.33}{26} = 0.40 \text{ p} \qquad \text{Whisky } \frac{7.40}{16} = 0.46 \text{ p}$$

Beverage cost is $0.40 + 0.46 = 0.86$ p.

$$\frac{\text{Beverage cost}}{\text{Beverage cost \%}} \times \frac{100}{1} = \text{Selling price}$$

$$\frac{0.86}{45} \times \frac{100}{1} = £1.91$$

Add VAT at 15 per cent:

$$\frac{15}{100} \times \frac{1.91}{1} = 0.29$$

Selling price of cocktail is $1.91 + 0.29 = $ **£2.20**

ASSIGNMENT

1. A keg of best bitter costs £42.20. Find the selling price of a pint inclusive of VAT if the publican seeks 44 per cent GP.
2. Find the selling price of a bottle of Pils lager if the crate of 24 bottles costs £8.56 and the bar is seeking a gross profit of 48 per cent.
3. If a restaurant buys Smirnoff vodka at £6.96 per bottle. Find the selling price per 6 fl.oz measure if a gross profit of 60 per cent is sought.
4. A club buys Remy Martin at £14.66 per bottle and seeks a gross profit of 40 per cent. Find the selling price per each '6 out' measure.
5. A restaurant seeks a gross profit of 35 per cent on a bottle of Chateau la Lagune costing £125 per case. Find the selling price.
6. A bottle of Rioja Berco Blanco cost £1.99 per bottle. A wine bar serving 4 fl.oz portions seeks a gross profit of 55 per cent. What would the selling price be?

7. Work out the selling price for a Bucks Fizz seeking a gross profit of 55 per cent.
8. Find the selling price of Brandy Alexander with a gross profit of 60 per cent.

PART III

13

EMPLOYMENT LEGISLATION

The law relating to employment is basically the law of contract. In its simplest terms a contract can be defined as a legally binding agreement enforceable by law. It exists through the specific intention of two sides to form a legal relationship. In the case of employment the contract exists as soon as a worker has agreed to the employer's terms and conditions of employment by starting work.

The **Employment Protection (Consolidation) Act 1978** (EPCA) and amended in 1980/82 deals with the bulk of employment legislation. Under this Act the employee is entitled, within 13 weeks of starting work, to be given a *written statement* containing terms of his/her employment, particularly with a note outlining disciplinary and grievance procedures.

The statement itself is not a contract but refers to the contract of employment. It is of course an important document in the event of a dispute. If there is no written contract of employment because the contract is a verbal one, the written statement can provide evidence on the terms and conditions of the verbal contract. The written statement must contain the names of both the employer and employee; the commencement date; whether employment with a previous employer counts as part of the employee's continuous employment; rate of pay or method of calculation; intervals at which payment falls due; hours of work; any terms or conditions concerning holidays, holiday pay, sickness or injury, pension scheme, length of notice required by either side to terminate the contract or date of termination in the case of a fixed-term contract, title of job and grade. In addition it must contain details of grievance procedures specifying the disciplinary rules and person to whom the employee can apply in case of dissatisfaction with a disciplinary decision.

Apart from matters which must be outlined in compliance with this Act, an employer may add other conditions, e.g. right to search, and conduct that would result in summary or instant dismissal, e.g. in catering, smoking in food-production areas may lead to instant dismissal.

It is not necessary for the employer to state in detail complicated terms provided the employee's attention is directed to reasonably accessible documents containing the necessary information. Any changes to the above conditions must be notified in writing within 4 weeks of the changes.

The obligation to provide the written particulars does not apply to those who normally work less than 16 hours per week unless they have been continuously employed by their employer for at least 5 years and for at least 8 hours per week. It does not apply either to independent contractors or freelance agents; those employed by the Crown; those employed wholly or mainly outside the UK; close relatives of the employer and those temporarily employed for less than 13 weeks.

Apart from any written terms in the contract, there are some common-sense rules known as 'implied terms' which are equally binding. These are obligations which the employee has towards the employer. Thus, on taking up employment an employee is expected to obey all lawful, reasonable and authorised instructions. An employee who persistently refuses to carry out the duties expected will be in breach of contract. He is not, however, obliged to obey orders that will involve any form of illegal or criminal activity.

Honesty at work is used in a broader context than just not stealing. Lateness and idleness, bribes (not to be confused with tips), activities detrimental to the employer's interest, using the employer's facilities for private gain, these are considered as breaches of contract. An employer is further entitled to include reasonable clauses preventing an employee on leaving the present employment, from entering a similar type of business.

An employee must exercise reasonable care and skill while carrying out duties. Negligence on the employee's part could lead to the employer calling on the employee to indemnify (i.e. to pay) the employer against damages payable to innocent third parties.

An employer owes certain duties to the employee. Unless there are any specific agreements the employer has the duty to remunerate, i.e. to pay the employee in cash. The employee is entitled (Section 8 of the EPCA) to an itemised pay statement. This must show the gross as well as the net 'take-home' pay with details and reasons for any deductions.

As a very general rule an employer is not under an obligation to provide work for an employee provided the agreed wages are paid. There are certain exceptions when the work has to be provided as well as the wages. However, this relates to the rules on lay-off which is outside the scope of this book.

An employee is entitled to be indemnified by the employer for any expenses, loss or liability incurred while undertaking work on behalf of the employer.

There is a widely implied duty on the employer to respect the employee. This means a certain amount of courtesy and consideration. A considerable number of unfair dismissals with its legal consequences could be avoided if the employer/employee relationships followed the Code of Practice issued by the Advisory Conciliation and Arbitration Service (ACAS). (A code of practice is not a set of binding rules but a list of suggestions conducive to a harmonious relationship.) An employer must not behave in such an unreasonable manner as to damage the confidence that should exist between employer and employee.

Under Sections 29, 30 and 32 of the EPCA, employees holding certain positions in public bodies are entitled to reasonable time off to perform those duties. These are positions like Justice of the Peace, member of local authorities, etc. The employer is not, however, obliged to pay the employee while absent attending these duties. Employees involved in shop steward's activities must be allowed time, with pay, to attend to trade-union activities.

An employer also has certain responsibilities towards the employees regarding their safety. These responsibilities are dealt with in more detail in Chapter 14.

REFERENCES

An employer is not obliged to provide any reference or testimonial on a former employee. The employer is also not obliged to deal with any queries or questions from a third party on an employee's character. When a reference is given it must be an honest one and free from malice as a false reference may bring consequences from either the employee or the third party seeking the reference.

DISMISSAL

The EPCA (Sections 78, 80, 82) gives most employees the right not to be unfairly dismissed. Dismissal means the termination of one's employment. The contract may be terminated by either party giving notice in accordance with the initial terms. In the absence of such terms the Act lays down that an employee is required to give the employer at least one week's notice if employed continuously for 1 month or more by that employer. The employer, however, is required to give an employee *1 week's notice* if the employee has been employed by that employer continuously for 1 month or more but less than 2 years, and at least 2 weeks' notice if the employee has been employed by the employer continuously for 2 years. One additional week's notice for each further complete year of continuous employment; and at least 12 weeks' notice if the employee has been employed by the employer for 12 years or more. An employer can give the equivalent wage in lieu of notice and is not bound to pay anything above the agreed wage.

Under the Act, an employer must accede within 14 days to a request from an employee for a written statement of reasons for dismissal. This is an important document if in the future it is needed as evidence.

A breach of contract by either party may allow the other party to terminate the contract. The breach must undermine the original purpose of the contract. The employer may dismiss an employee, although of course the employee has certain recourse against the employer and can complain if unfairly dismissed to an industrial tribunal (see below).

There are five basic reasons which may justify dismissal:
1. Misconduct;
2. Frustration;
3. Redundancy;
4. Illegality;
5. Some other substantial reason.

MISCONDUCT

What degree of misconduct justifies dismissal is difficult to state, but generally it would be a type of behaviour which would frequently impair the employee's recognised performance of his duties. As a guideline, the degree of careful behaviour expected of the employee increases with the degree of responsibility which the job covers. Wilful disobedience may also lead to dismissal. Again, circumstances are important but as a guideline, an unwarranted refusal to obey a lawful order or wilfully neglecting to carry out an agreed task could be grounds. The employee, of course, may complain to an industrial tribunal. The industrial tribunal would, however, probably ask whether the employee knew that an offence was being committed, and whether the employee had previously been warned for a similar offence. The tribunal would also probably want to know whether the employee was given the opportunity of explaining reasons for such behaviour. It would want to ensure that the facts had been thoroughly investigated prior to dismissal.

FRUSTRATION

When fundamental changes occur that make performance in its original form impossible the contract becomes frustrated, that is, it cannot continue in existence. Common reasons that frustrate the contract of employment are inability to do the job, particularly through illness or imprisonment. An employer, however, needs caution before dismissing for any of these reasons since recent cases have been found to be unfair dismissal. If an employee brings a case for unfair dismissal to an industrial tribunal on any of these grounds the tribunal would probably enquire whether the employee had been given adequate training, received adequate supervision, had been told to make an effort to improve or been previously warned. The tribunal might also enquire whether the employee was properly selected for the job.

When it comes to ill health the tribunal recognises that small employers are unable to keep jobs open indefinitely, but nevertheless would probably like to find out whether the employer had discussed the situation with the employee or the possibility of shorter hours or different work.

A term of imprisonment may well terminate the contract. However, a tribunal would probably wish to consider the length of imprisonment, the commercial consequences for the firm and whether a temporary replacement was possible. Criminal offences unrelated to the job are not necessarily grounds for dismissal.

REDUNDANCY

It is fair to dismiss employees because fewer people are needed. However, the employer must show that the selection was fair and that there was no prejudice. There are detailed provisions in law for handling redundancies. The redundant employee has certain basic rights that the employer must meet. Amongst these is the right to reasonable time off with pay to seek another job.

ILLEGALITY

If the continued employment of an employee resulted in the employer breaking the law, the dismissal would be fair. For example, a driver who has been disqualified from driving, or a foreign worker with an expired work permit.

SOME OTHER SUBSTANTIAL REASON

Any good and fair reason for dismissal not covered under the above headings will be considered by a tribunal. A common reason under this heading is difficult staff relationships, i.e. someone with whom the staff had great difficulty in getting on. Another is when reasonable and unavoidable changes to current duties or conditions are unacceptable to the employee. An employee may be dismissed if the details on an application form are found to be false. Also when business reorganisation makes it necessary to dispense with an employee, although most cases here would come under redundancy regulations. There are also regulations to cover a dismissal as a result of the transfer of a business. A replacement worker, may, however, be dismissed after the return of the original worker. This happens when a replacement has been found while a worker is away over a long absence.

FAIR OR UNFAIR DISMISSAL

As can be seen, the manner in which a dismissal is handled can change a fair dismissal into an unfair one. There are, however, certain grounds on which a dismissal is automatically unfair. This happens when an employee is dismissed:
(a) For belonging to a union or taking part in union activities;
(b) When the employer has not followed the agreed or customary procedures in the selection of personnel for redundancy;
(c) When the dismissal is associated with pregnancy;
(d) Through the transfer of business to a new employer;
(e) Breaches of the Race Relations Act 1976;
(f) Contravention of the Sex Discrimination Act 1975;
(g) Recent directives from Government indicate that dismissal because of the 'AIDS' virus is unfair.

CONSTRUCTIVE DISMISSAL

It is possible for an employee to resign on the grounds that the employer's conduct was such that the employee felt entitled to terminate the contract. This is known as constructive dismissal. The employee may bring an action for unfair dismissal. Although an employee may have been constructively dismissed entitlement to compensation is not automatic. The employee must show that the dismissal was unfair.

ASSIGNMENT

1. In which year did the Employment Protection (Consolidation) Act become law?
2. Within how many weeks of commencement of employment must a written statement be issued?
3. List six requirements which must be included in the written statement.
4. Could an employer include a right-to-search condition in the contract of employment?
5. Give two examples of employed persons who are not entitled to a written statement.
6. Explain the meaning of 'implied terms' in a contract of employment.
7. How much dismissal notice is Bill Booth entitled to if he has worked for his current employer for 27 months?
8. Jack Roberts claims he is entitled to time off with pay because as a member of the Northern Regional Health Authority he has to attend meetings. State whether he is correct or not, giving reasons for your answer.
9. List five reasons that may justify dismissal.
10. Explain briefly the term 'constructive dismissal'.
11. While emptying a cauldron of hot stock, the cauldron slipped and John, a commis chef, had both legs very badly burned. John successfully gained compensation from his employers, City Metro Hotel. According to the sous-chef who was nearby when the accident happened, John was hurt because Peter, another commis chef who was helping John, was 'fooling around'. Advise the employers whether or not they could call upon Peter to indemnify them against the compensation they had to pay John.
12. Fred was employed for about three months at the Bellevue

Hotel. As an ardent trade unionist he was anxious to recruit other staff to the union. During most tea and lunch breaks Fred would persuade colleagues to join him. The manager asked him to stop this daily activity which he claimed was causing 'much unhappiness among staff'. Fred refused to stop his activities and was fired. Comment whether or not Fred is protected by the current employment legislation.

INDUSTRIAL TRIBUNALS

A dismissed employee may put a claim against the employer on the grounds that the dismissal was unfair. The employee (the applicant) must then make an application to an industrial tribunal (on Form IT1) as soon as the employer (the respondent) has given notice of dismissal. The application which gives particulars of the complaint must be made within 3 months of the date of termination. A late application will be considered only in exceptional circumstances. A copy of the form is then sent to the employer (Notice of Appearance). The employer must reply stating whether the case is to be contested or not and giving grounds for doing so. Before any hearing takes place an opportunity is provided for conciliation. This is done by an officer from ACAS (which is totally independent from the tribunal). The ACAS officer tries to get the applicant and the respondent to reach a voluntary agreement without going to the tribunal. Many cases are settled in this way, usually with an agreed sum of money in compensation. If no settlement is possible then the matter proceeds for hearing by the tribunal.

The industrial tribunal is a court of law which limits its business to matters of employment only. However, cases are dealt with more casually than in a traditional court-room because procedures before a tribunal are simple and designed to give easy access to lay people. Although many parties are legally represented, that is, have lawyers with them at the hearing, most cases are conducted by the parties themselves. The tribunal has no judges but is presided over by a chairman who is a legally qualified person and two other members, one appointed after consultation with employers' associations and the other after consultation with employees' associations. Tribunals sit in larger towns and cities throughout the country.

At the tribunal the clerk explains the procedure to the parties before the case begins. The chairman also assists both parties since tribunals try to keep their proceedings as simple and informal as possible. Both parties put forward their cases and both can question each other and witnesses. If one party does not attend the hearing the tribunal may rule in its absence. However, the tribunal may dismiss an application if the applicant fails to attend without an explanation. Tribunal hearings are normally completed in a day. Decisions may be by majority vote, though in practice most are unanimous. The decision and reasons are usually announced straight away. A copy of the written decision is sent to both parties within 2 months and either party has a right to ask for a review or to appeal to the Employment Appeal Tribunal on a point of law.

If the dismissal is found to be fair the application will be dismissed. If the dismissal is found to be unfair the tribunal can order:

1. *Reinstatement*. The employer may be ordered to reinstate the employee in the same job. Before making the order the tribunal considers the employee's wishes; the practicality of that employee returning to work and in cases where the employee may have contributed to the dismissal whether it would be just to make such an order.
2. *Re-engagement*. This is an order for the employer to re-engage the employee in a different job. The same criteria as for reinstatement applies.
3. *Compensation*. The employer may be ordered to pay a sum of money to the employee in compensation. This is calculated at $1\frac{1}{2}$ week's pay for every year continuous employment for those between 41 and 65; 1 week's pay for those between 22 and 40; and $\frac{1}{2}$ week's pay for those under 22. The maximum number of weeks is 30.

For unfair dismissals connected with trade-union activities or through redundancy reasons, the basic award will normally be a minimum of £2,000.

The award may be reduced if the employee contributed to the dismissal or has already received redundancy payment. A compensatory award may be given if the employee suffered loss as a result of the dismissal.

If the employer fails to comply with a reinstatement or re-engagement order a compensation award is made together with an additional award, minimum 13 weeks pay and a maximum of 26 weeks' pay. For dismissals in breach of either the Sex Discrimination Act 1975 or the Race Relations Act 1976 the additional award is for a minimum of 26 weeks and a maximum of 52 weeks.

TRADE UNIONS

The hotel and catering industry is a large one employing almost 10 per cent of the country's workforce, yet membership of trade unions is one of the lowest. Many of the problems that management encounter in industrial relations are ironically some of the same causes why the unionisation of the workers in this industry has been so difficult.

A large proportion of the hotel and catering workers are casual or seasonal. This type of employee is less likely to value the advantages of union membership than a full-time employee in respect to job protection, wage increases, etc. The industry employs many women, the majority married mothers. While women's attitudes are changing, traditionally women in general have been less inclined to take part in union activities. Labour turnover is very high, and although very costly to the industry it is generally accepted as normal by management. Only a small proportion of the industry's establishments belong to or are large organisations. The majority are relatively small individual hotels, restaurants and canteens widely spread, thus making control of employment practices difficult. Small family (self-employed) units predominate in the industry and these are very unlikely to show any interest in trade unions. The nature of the work itself, departmentalisation and shifts, makes labour organisation difficult. The hotel and catering industry is a service industry. The majority of those choosing to join have a conscientious instinct to service. This would prevent them from taking any action which could remotely affect that service to customers. Many of the staff are foreign with language and cultural difficulties. These may also be less likely to join unions. There are still many employers who are suspicious of unions and who have reservations about encouraging staff to join unions.

These are some causes why trade union membership in the hotel and catering industry is still relatively low. However, indications are that membership is gradually growing. Some employers are now encouraging staff to join and are beginning to recognise unions.

Trade unions aim to represent and advance the interests of their members. This is performed through the close liaison of shop stewards at shop-floor level and full-time paid union officials at the respective union's headquarters. Unions have 'back-up' facilities for research, legal assistance and for carrying out complex negotiations. The main unions operating in the hotel and catering industry are the Transport and General Workers Union; General and Municipal Workers Union; Transport Salaried Staffs Association; National Union of Railwaymen; Union of Shop Distributive and Allied Workers; National Association of Licensed House Managers.

14

HEALTH, SAFETY AND HYGIENE

There are a variety of laws affecting the hotel and catering industry, but as this chapter deals with health and safety and hygiene it would be appropriate to consider the Health and Safety at Work Act 1974 and the Food Act 1984.

THE HEALTH AND SAFETY AT WORK ACT 1974

This Act, commonly referred to as HASWA, consists of very extensive regulations covering all aspects of health and safety affecting employees and the general public. It is a most important piece of legislation which even affects firms employing only one person. The Act tidied up, by adding to and partially replacing, previous work-related legislation. The Act extended the scope of health and safety legislation to *all* persons at work, except domestic servants in private households. It brought protection, for the first time, to millions employed in industries not previously covered.

Section 1 of the Act sets out its objectives. It aims to secure the health, safety and welfare of all persons at work and also at protecting other persons not at work against possible hazards created by those at work. It exercises control over explosive, highly inflammable and dangerous substances and equipment as well as the emission into the atmosphere of noxious or offensive substances.

The general duties of employers to their employees is contained in **Section 2** of the Act by clearly stating: 'It shall be the duty of every employer to ensure, so far as is reasonably practicable, the health, safety and welfare at work of all his employees.' So far as is reasonably practicable, this implies weighing up the seriousness of a risk against the difficulty and cost of removing it. In some cases, however, for health and safety reasons, things have to be done at all costs, no matter what the size, nature or profitability of the business.

Section 2 also lays down the employer's responsibility to ensure that all plant and machinery are safe and without risk to health. This implies the proper inspection, maintenance and repair of equipment and appliances, not only with regard to use but also to handling, storage and transport. It lays down the need for suitable training. It also requires the employer to ensure that all possible care is taken to avoid obstructing corridors and stairways and to provide easy access through doors and exits.

Also under Section 2 any employer with more than five employees must write and keep up to date a **Safety Policy Statement**. The statement is the employer's basic action plan on health and safety which all managers and employees should read, understand and follow. It must describe the organisation and arrangements for carrying out the policy and must be revised whenever appropriate and every revision brought to the attention of the employees. The section also provides for the arrangement of a safety representative and of safety committees.

Section 3 deals with duties of the employer towards persons not being employees. Section 3(1): 'It shall be the duty of every employer to conduct his undertakings in such a way as to ensure, so far as it is reasonably practicable, that persons not in his employment who may be affected thereby are not thereby exposed to risks to their health and safety.' Section 3(2) is similar but applies to the duties of a self-employed person. Section 3(3) places a duty on an employer to give information to persons, not being employees, but who may be affected by the conduct of his undertakings or the aspects of his undertakings, as may affect the health and safety of those persons.

Under **Section 6** the employer becomes liable for defects in any equipment which he supplies to his employees for the purpose of their work. The employer is further responsible for carrying out or arranging to be carried out such testing or examination as is necessary to ensure the safe use of equipment and without risks to health. He must also ensure proper training in the use of such equipment and is further responsible for the proper installation of any such equipment.

Each individual employee – and it must be noted that members of management may be employees within the meaning of the Act – will be rendered liable, under pain of prosecution, to ensure his own health and safety as well as that of his colleagues. Thus under **Section 7** carelessness and 'fooling around' can have serious consequences. **Section 8** places a duty on all persons and states: 'no person shall intentionally or recklessly interfere with or misuse anything provided in the interests of health, safety or welfare in pursuance of any of the relevant statutory provisions'. To do so is a criminal offence punishable by a £1,000 fine in a magistrates' court or an unlimited fine in a Crown Court.

Section 9 of the Act prohibits employers from levying on an employee any charge in respect of anything done or provided in pursuance of any specific requirement of any of the legislation for health, safety and welfare. In other words the employer must provide free, any protective clothing or equipment required by law.

The Act establishes two institutions, the Health and Safety Commission and the Health and Safety Executive. The Health and Safety Commission was set up under **Section 10** of the Act, making it primarily responsible for administering the law and practice of health and safety at work.

The Commission must make arrangements to fulfil the general aim of the Act as set out in Section 1 which requires 'securing the health, safety and welfare of persons at work and protecting persons other than persons at work against risk to health or safety arising out of or in connection with the activities of persons at work'. It consists of representatives from both sides of industry and local authorities. It is responsible for the policies of health and safety and under **Section 14** has powers to order an investigation or inquiry.

The Health and Safety Executive is a separate statutory body appointed by the Commission to work in accordance with the Commission's directions and guidance.

The Executive will also enforce legal requirements as well as provide an advisory service to both sides of industry.

The Act is enforced through an inspectorate. For most industrial businesses the inspectors will come from the Health and Safety Executive. Restaurants and hotels, together with offices, shops and warehouses are the responsibility of the local authorities. Their health and safety inspectors are usually in the council's environmental health department.

The powers enabling an inspector to undertake the duties under the Act are given in **Section 20**. These include power to enter any premises at any reasonable time and if need be bring along with him any duly authorised person and equipment that may be considered necessary for any examination or investigation. The inspector may take samples and require any person to give information relevant to the examination or investigation. Any person may be required to afford the inspector such facilities and assistance, within that person's control or responsibilities, as are necessary to enable the inspector to exercise any of the powers conferred on him.

The Act is more concerned with prevention than with punishment. The first approach to enforcement is through advice and assistance from the inspectors to those who have to meet the requirements of the Act. If an inspector discovers a contravention of one of the provisions of the existing Act or regulations, he can issue a *Prohibition Notice* if there is a risk of personal serious injury. Its purpose is to stop the activity giving rise to the risk until remedial action specified in the notice has been taken. The notice can be issued whether or not there is a legal contravention, and it can take effect immediately or at a later time. It can be served on the person undertaking the activity or on a person in control of it at the time the notice was served.

If there is a legal contravention of any of the relevant statutory provisions, the inspector may issue an *Improvement Notice* to remedy the fault within a specified time. This notice will be served on the person who is deemed to be contravening the legal provisions or it can be served on any person on whom responsibility is placed, whether it be an employer, employed person or a supplier of equipment and material. A person on whom a notice is served may appeal against it, or any terms of it, to an industrial tribunal.

The inspector may prosecute in very serious cases or for non-compliance with notices. Cases are brought to court by the Health and Safety Executive. Fines imposed by a Crown Court can be unlimited and for certain serious cases imprisonment for up to 2 years. In addition to any other penalty, the court can make an order requiring the cause of the offence to be remedied.

An inspector is also empowered to seize, render harmless or destroy any substance or article that may be considered to be the cause of imminent danger or serious personal injury.

Accidents and dangerous occurrences resulting from work activities covered by HASWA are to be reported under the Notification of Accidents and Dangerous Occurrences Regulations 1980. These regulations deal with incidents involving a *fatal accident* whether the victim is an employee, guest or visitor. This must be reported to the local authority. A *major injury* involving loss of limb must also be reported. Whether or not there has been injury, all *dangerous occurrences*, e.g. explosions or fires, must be reported. Any *other accident* must be recorded but not reported. Reports are to be made by the quickest means available.

The Prescribed Dangerous Machines Order 1964 classifies dangerous machines, among which are those typically found in the catering industry. Young persons under 18 must not use dangerous machines except under qualified supervision.

I. Power-driven machines – the following types
1. Worm-type mixing machines;
2. Rotary knife bowl-type chopping machines;
4. Dough mixers;
5. Food-mixing machines when used with attachments for mincing, slicing, chipping and any other cutting operations or for crumbling;
6. Pie- and tart-making machines;
7. Vegetable-slicing machines.

II. Machines whether or not power driven
17. Circular knife slicing machines used for cutting bacon and other foods (whether or not similar to bacon);
18. Potato-chipping machines.

The Act is drafted in general terms and every employer must consider within the context of his own organisation the necessary action required to comply with the duties demanded of him by the Act. As the wording is not specific, 'Health' seems to imply the physical and mental health of employees whereas 'Safety' appears to imply the absence or prevention of injury. Section 2(1) also implies that welfare might be interpreted as referring to the personal comfort of employees.

It must be remembered that HASWA 1974 replaces parts of earlier Acts but does not supersede the detailed requirements contained in the earlier legislation. Therefore the Factories Act 1961; the Offices, Shops and Railways Act 1963; the Employers' Liability (Compulsory Insurance) Act 1969 and the Fire Precautions Act 1971 are still in force.

SUMMARY

1. The Act places duties on employers, employees and the general public.
2. It seeks to prevent rather than punish.
3. It lays responsibilities for:
   (a) a safe work-place;
   (b) safe levels of dust, fumes and noise;
   (c) safety standards for use of equipment.

4. Provisions for adequate training on safety.
5. Establishes worker safety representatives.
6. Provides inspectors with powers of enforcement.

ASSIGNMENT

1. Explain briefly the aim of HASWA 1974.
2. What major responsibilities does this Act place on employers?
3. What is the minimum number of employees before a safety policy statement must be written?
4. Which are the institutions established under Section 10 of the Act?
5. Through whom is the Act enforced?
6. Explain powers which are available under Section 20 of the Act.
7. Explain briefly the difference between an Improvement Notice and a Prohibition Notice.
8. What is the maximum penalty a Crown Court may impose for serious contravention of the Act.
9. Describe briefly the requirements of the Notification of Accidents and Dangerous Occurrences Regulations 1980.
10. Give five examples of catering equipment listed under the Dangerous Machines Order 1964.
11. Make a list of areas likely to be checked by a Health and Safety Inspector visiting a hotel kitchen.
12. Assuming you have been selected as representative to sit on the hotel's Safety Committee, what sort of points would you like to see included in a safety policy?

THE FOOD ACT 1984

This Act seeks to protect consumers from impure and unwholesome food and provides penalties for persons guilty of offences under the Act. The Act consolidated much of the previous legislation on this subject and provides for hygienic standards to be enforced in premises where food is either stored, prepared or served.

It is a large and rather complicated piece of legislation drawn up into seven parts. It relates mainly to food saleable for human consumption but also deals with dairies; markets; hawkers; sugar-beet; registration and inspection of goods and premises; and with labelling regulations.

Section 1 deals with the preparation and sales of injurious foods. In the simplest terms the section forbids any form of food adulteration or the selling of food whether adulterated by the seller or a third party. Further, it is an offence to offer, expose or advertise for sale for human consumption or even be in possession, for the purpose of possible sale, of any food rendered injurious to health. Under **Section 8** any doubts are eradicated by the provisions contained in this section which makes it a criminal offence to sell any food intended for, but unfit for, human consumption. Prosecution is directed towards the retailer of food products, and towards the wholesaler, manufacturer and transporter of food products.

Section 2 provides general protection for the purchaser of food. If a person sells to the prejudice of the purchaser any food which is not of the nature, or not of the substance, or not of the quality, of the food demanded by the purchaser, that person shall be guilty of an offence.

Under **Section 4** ministers may make regulations concerning any process or treatment of food, requiring, prohibiting or regulating additives and generally regulating the composition of food. There are already in effect a considerable number of these regulations.

Section 6 makes it an offence to sell a food with a label or advertise a food in a way that either falsely decribes the food or is calculated to mislead as to the nature, substance or quality (including nutritional or dietary value) of the food.

The minister responsible is empowered under **Section 7** to issue regulations imposing requirements and regulating the labelling, marking or advertising of food and the descriptions applied to food (excluding milk). There are a number of labelling regulations in force, but the bulk goes under the Food Labelling Regulations 1984. It is impossible in a book of this kind to go into detail, but the general labelling requirements are that all food should be marked with the name of the food and a list of ingredients. It must also give an indication of minimum durability and any special storage conditions or conditions of use. The name and address of either manufacturer or packer or seller must be marked, the place of origin if necessary to avoid misleading the purchaser and instructions for use if necessary.

Section 9 provides for an authorised officer of a council to inspect food and if in his opinion any food appears unfit for human consumption he has power to seize and remove the suspected food in order that it may be dealt with by a Justice of the Peace who may condemn it and order it to be destroyed. The owner of the food may appear before the Justice of the Peace and bring witnesses with him. Should the Justice of the Peace refuse to condemn the food the council shall compensate the owner for any depreciation in value.

The responsible minister is empowered by **Section 13** of the Act to issue regulations to ensure that sanitary and clean conditions and practices are observed in connection with the sale of food or the importation, preparation, transport, storage, packaging, wrapping, exposure for sale, service or delivery of food intended for sale or sold for human consumption or otherwise for the protection of the public health.

The regulations currently in force are the Food Hygiene (General) Regulations 1970. These lay down hygiene standards for all premises concerned with the preparation and sale of food whether or not for profit and includes canteens, clubs, schools, hospitals or institutions and any undertaking carried on by a public or local authority.

The main aspects of the regulations are as follows:

1. No food business may be carried on at any insanitary premises or in any situation that may expose food to the risk of contamination.
2. All articles and equipment with which food comes into contact shall be kept clean and designed to enable them to be thoroughly cleaned to prevent contamination.
3. Food shall be protected from contamination, not positioned to involve risk and separated from food which is unfit for human consumption.
4. To prevent contamination, food kept in an open space must be at least 18 in from the ground. Open food must be adequately covered or screened during delivery or sale and animal feed must be kept in separate rooms.
5. Anyone handling food must keep clean all parts of the person and clothing likely to come into contact with food. All exposed cuts or abrasions must be covered with waterproof dressing. Spitting or smoking in food-production areas is strictly forbidden.
6. Food handlers, except waiters, should wear clean and washable over-clothing and the employer must provide accommodation for storing the clothing away from food areas.
7. Food cannot be wrapped in any unclean material or printed paper.
8. Any food handler who is suspected to be suffering from or may be carrying any infectious disease must refrain from

working near food and must notify a medical officer. A first-aid kit must always be available.

9. The employer must provide clean washing and toilet facilities which, apart from clean water and towels, also includes soap and a nail-brush. Notices requiring staff to wash their hands after using the toilet must be displayed.

10. All food-preparation rooms must be well lit and ventilated and kept clean and in a good state of repair to discourage insects.

11. There must be an adequate water supply to food-preparation rooms and an efficient drainage system and proper facilities for washing food and equipment separately.

12. Accumulation of refuse beyond that which is reasonably necessary is not allowed and proper provisions must exist for the removal of refuse.

13. The regulations also set out temperatures at which certain catering foods must be kept.

14. While the regulations in themselves do not exclude dogs from food premises, it is, however, arguable whether they are permitted since 'food must be protected from risk of contamination'. It would be reasonable, therefore, to assume that dogs are not allowed in food premises.

Section 9 of the Food Act 1984 gives powers of entry and of inspection and seizure of suspect foods to the environmental health officers of the local council. These officials are also responsible for the prosecution of offences against the regulations and upon their application, the magistrate's court may, under **Section 14**, make an order disqualifying a person from using or managing premises for catering purposes for a period not exceeding 2 years. However, any time after 6 months of the order's effective date the person may apply for the order to be lifted. If after consideration the court is satisfied, the application may be granted.

Sections 21 to 26 deal with control of premises and the local authority may apply to the court for a closure order if the offence includes carrying on a food business at any insanitary premises or under such insanitary conditions that the food is exposed to the risk of contamination. If the court is satisfied that the situation will continue and that because of the insanitary conditions there would be a danger to public health, the court may issue the closure order prohibiting the continuation of the business until the local authority certifies that the danger to health has been removed. Fourteen days' notice is necessary under the Act before the court takes action. If, however, the court is satisfied that the danger to health is imminent then an emergency order is granted prohibiting the business from continuing. An emergency order requires only 3 days' notice. In practice, however, the process of reopening is both complex and costly as the backing of the local authority and endorsement of the court is required.

Offences are divided by **Sections 92** and **93** into those tried summarily (i.e. in a magistrates' court) and those which are more serious and may be tried summarily or on indictment (i.e. at a Crown Court).

The magistrates' court may fine a guilty person up to £2,000. In the Crown Court the penalty may consist of an unlimited fine and/or up to 2 years' imprisonment.

Under **Section 91** any person obstructing an officer carrying out his duties under the Act commits an offence.

Under **Sections 104** and **105** appeals against a refusal or other decision of a local authority are allowed to be made at magistrates' courts. Appeals against decisions of magistrates' courts can be made at a Crown Court.

With effect from 7 February 1987 hospital kitchens lost their Crown immunity as their privileged status has been abolished under the National Health Service (Amendment) Act 1986. Hospital managers who allow poor hygiene in their kitchens will suffer the same penalties as any commercial establishment.

SUMMARY

1. The Food Act 1984 protects the consumer's health and imposes penalties for breaches of the Act.
2. The local environmental health officer can inspect, seize and remove offensive food.
3. Under Section 13 of the Act, the Food Hygiene (General) Regulations are in force which deal with hygiene matters relating to products, premises, processes and people.
4. Environmental health officers inspect premises and issue Improvement Notices instructing owners to rectify hygiene problems.
5. The courts are empowered under the Act to:
   (a) disqualify a person from using or managing premises for catering purposes;
   (b) issue a closure order after 14 days' notice;
   (c) issue an emergency order after 3 days' notice.

15

LICENSING AND TRADE DESCRIPTION

The licensing legislation in this country is both cumbersome and complicated. It would be beyond the scope of this book other than to give a brief résumé of the requirements of the Licensing Act 1964.

LICENCES

The law forbids the retail sale of intoxicating liquor for consumption on or off the premises unless under the authority of a licence. The licence is known as a 'Justices' Licence' because it is granted at licensing sessions held during the year by local Justices of the Peace.

There are basically two types of Justices' Licence:
1. An 'on-licence' (sometimes known as a full licence or full-on licence). This authorises the sale of intoxicating liquor which may be consumed either on or off the premises.
2. An 'off-licence' which permits the sale of intoxicating liquor for consumption off the premises only. Each type of licence falls into categories. The on-licence has five categories and the off-licence has two.

THE ON-LICENCE

The five categories are:
1. Intoxicating liquor of all descriptions;
2. Beer, cider and wine only;
3. Beer and cider only;
4. Cider only;
5. Wine only.

The Justices have wide powers and can attach, to any licence, conditions that they may think proper in the interests of the public. These could deal, for example, with structural matters like fire escapes, access or suitability of certain parts of the premises. Conditions may also be imposed under various sections of the Act. These may be for example, no permitted hours on a Sunday (six-day licence); closing an hour earlier every evening (early-closing licence); opening at certain times of the year only, suitable for holiday resorts (seasonal licence). There are, of course, various legal technicalities attached to these which would be outside the scope of this book. It would, however, follow from the above that the most useful and practicable licence to apply for would be the full-on licence for the sale of intoxicating liquor of all descriptions. In practice this is the most difficult to obtain and many applications are turned down annually.

THE OFF-LICENCE

The two categories are:
1. Intoxicating liquor of all descriptions;
2. Beer, cider and wine.

These authorise the sale of liquor to anyone over 18 years old for consumption off the premises. There are no other restrictions that the Justices may impose on this type of licence. The Justices may, however, in the interest of the public suspend the automatic right to make off-sales which is available under an on-licence. Off-licences allow longer opening hours and many of these sales are carried out in supermarkets. Under **Section 164** it is an offence to sell from an off-licence premises wines or spirits in an open container.

PART IV LICENCES

In order to allow hotels and restaurants to supply intoxicating liquor the Licensing Act 1961 made provisions under its Part IV for this purpose. This was later incorporated into the 1964 Act and have become known as Part IV licences. These consist of: (1) The residential licence; (2) the restaurant licence; (3) the residential and restaurant licence (sometimes referred to as the combined licence).

Residential licence
The Licensing Act 1964 defines a *residential licence* as being granted for 'premises bona fide used, or intended to be used, for the purpose of habitually providing for reward, board and lodging,

including breakfast and one other, at least, of the customary main meals'. The condition limits the sale of liquor to persons residing on the premises and to their bona fide guests provided the residing person pays. The requirements also state that a room, completely free from the supply or consumption of liquor, must be available. Justices do not always impose the 'dry room' (as it is commonly known) requirement. An implied condition in all Part IV licences is that a suitable non-intoxicating beverage is available to be served with meals. Provided these conditions are adhered to there are no 'permitted hours' in force. The requirement of 'one other main meal' excludes bed-and-breakfast establishments from acquiring this licence.

Restaurant licence

The Act also defines the *restaurant licence* as being granted 'for premises structurally adapted and bona fide used, or intended to be used, for the purpose of habitually providing the customary main meal at midday or in the evening, or both, for the accommodation of persons frequenting the premises and subject to the condition that intoxicating liquor shall not be supplied on the premises otherwise than to persons taking table meals there and for consumption by such persons as an ancillary to his meal'. This means that customers cannot 'pop-in' for a drink. Drinks can be served away from the table provided they are part of the meal. The grant of this licence automatically allows the sale of liquor with meals until 3 p.m. daily. The evening hours can be extended through a Supper Hour Certificate (see below). The Justices may refuse to grant a restaurant licence if they believe the premises will be patronised largely by unaccompanied under-18s or if a substantial proportion of the business will be on a self-service basis with liquor being sold.

Residential and restaurant licence

As its name implies, this is a combination of two licences. It is suitable for a small hotel which may open its restaurant, but not the bar, to the public. The licence is subject to the restrictions imposed by both the residential licence and the restaurant licence.

A person who already holds an on-licence may be granted an *occasional licence* for the purpose of selling liquor at some special event to be held at unlicensed premises. This is not a full licence but some kind of extension to an existing licence. It is granted for any period of up to three weeks and is usually for such occasions as balls or fêtes. When granted the licence will indicate the actual hours when sale of liquor may be made, but it will be free from any restrictions which may have been included in the holder's full-on licence.

PERMITTED HOURS

Section 59 of the 1964 Act makes it an offence for either the licensee, i.e. the licence holder, or a representative of the holder, to sell or supply intoxicating liquor outside permitted hours. It is also an offence for a customer to consume intoxicating liquor in the premises outside permitted hours. The licensee cannot entertain guests outside the permitted hours even at the licensee's expense; nor is it legal for either the licensee, staff or family to purchase or consume liquor. The premises, however, are not required to close at the end of permitted hours provided no liquor is sold or supplied.

Section 60 deals with the permitted hours for on-licence premises, which are:

Metropolitan area: (i.e. Inner London or City of London)	Weekdays	Sundays, Christmas Day and Good Friday
	11 a.m. to 3 p.m. 5.30 p.m. to 11 p.m.	Noon to 2 p.m. 7 p.m. to 10.30 p.m.
Outside Metropolitan	11 a.m. to 3 p.m. 5.30 p.m. to 10.30 p.m.	Noon to 2 p.m. 7 p.m. to 10.30 p.m.

The permitted hours for off-sales are between 8.30 a.m. and 11 p.m. on weekdays; on Sundays, Christmas Day and Good Friday, noon to 2 p.m. and 7 p.m. to 10.30 p.m.

The basic permitted hours which are set out may be varied or amended in a number of ways provided for in the Act.

EXEMPTIONS

Under **Section 74** a *General Order of Exemption* may be granted to the holder of an on-licence whose premises are situated in the immediate neighbourhood of a local market or the locality of people following a lawful trade or calling where such an order is desirable to accommodate them for the purpose of refreshment during times when the licensed premises would be closed.

Under the same section, a *Special Order of Exemption* may be granted which effectively permits an extension of normal permitted hours of an on-licence premises for a special occasion. It must be for a specific occasion not one on a regular basis. Numerous cases have dealt with the difficult question of what is or is not a special occasion for the purpose of this section. General guidelines are that it must be of national or local significance; that it must be for the benefit of those participating in the national or local event; and that it must not be so frequent as to appear regular.

A *Supper Hour Certificate* may be granted under **Section 68** provided the Justices are satisfied that the licensed premises are structurally adapted and that they are bona fide used or intended to be used for providing, on a regular basis, substantial refreshment to which the sale and supply of intoxicating liquor is ancillary. It is left to the Justices' discretion as to whether the extension will apply to both lunch-time and evening. Such extensions apply only to those parts of the premises set aside for the service of table meals. The effect of this is to enable liquor to be served for a further hour. The certificate continues in force without need for renewal, but may be withdrawn at any time if the premises cease to qualify under the conditions laid down.

An establishment which qualifies for a Supper Hour Certificate may in addition be granted an *Extended Hours Order* under **Section 70** of the Act. This in effect extends the permitted hours to 1 a.m. on certain days of the week. In order for the Extended Hours Order to be granted the premises must show that not only do they qualify for a Supper Hour Certificate but that the sale of the intoxicating liquor is ancillary to the supply of substantial refreshment and live entertainment. The sale of liquor must cease when the meals and entertainment stop, though in any case, it must finish by 1 a.m.

Section 76 provides for the granting of *Special Hours Certificates* where the sale of liquor accompanies and is ancillary to the service of substantial refreshment and the provision of music and dancing facilities. The permitted hours under the issue of this certificate are 12.30 p.m. to 3.00 p.m. and 6.30 p.m. to 2.00 a.m. (3.00 a.m. in Central London). Whenever the certificate is applied the police must be notified. When music and dancing ends between midnight and 2 a.m. the permitted hours also end.

After the end of permitted hours 10 minutes' *drinking-up time* is allowed for drinking up liquor which had already been purchased. Drinking-up time is 30 minutes when it applies to liquor bought ancillary to meals. It is also 30 minutes when any of the above-mentioned exemption orders or extension certificates are in force.

YOUNG PERSONS

It is an offence for a licensee to *knowingly* sell liquor to a person under 18 years of age, to allow such a person to consume liquor in a bar or to allow someone else to buy on behalf of the under-18. A person aged over 16 may purchase and consume beer, porter, cider or perry as part of a meal in an area of the building which is not a bar. No under-14 may be present in a bar during the permitted hours, though this excludes the licensee's own child or resident child not employed at the premises. A child is, however, allowed to pass through a bar, e.g. to use the toilet. A licensee is committing an offence by employing an under-18 in the bar during the sale or consumption of liquor. The Act assumes the person is employed even though there may be no payment of wages. Other sections of the Act make provisions for exceptions when the dispensing of liquor is in connection with table meals or if the person normally works in another part of the building. In short, an under-18 can be a waiter but not a barperson, and, a person undertaking reception duties may be allowed freely to enter or pass through the bar in the execution of those duties.

APPLYING FOR LICENCES

New licences must be obtained and existing ones renewed or may be transferred. Any of these three actions need to be carried out under the authority of the local Licensing Justices formed from the Bench of the local Justices of the Peace. The Justices hold an Annual Licensing Meeting in the first fortnight in February. In addition they hold between four and eight licensing sessions during the year. The meeting and sessions are advertised in the local press about a month before. Each licensing authority has a clerk to the Justices who deals with all the administration in connection with licences.

In the case of a new licence the applicant must notify the clerk to the Justices, the chief of police, the fire authority and the local authority of the application no less than 21 days prior to the licensing meeting and must conveniently display a notice outside the premises to that effect (this must be done for 7 days within a period of 28 days). Between 14 and 28 days prior to the hearing, a notice must be displayed in the local press. The notice is in standard form, but in any case must state the applicant's name, address and occupation and the type of licence being applied for. The applicant must attend the licensing session in person though legal representation is permitted.

Licences must be renewed annually as they expire on 4 April. Licences are normally renewed *en bloc* at the annual meeting, but it is nevertheless the responsibility of the holder to ensure that the licence is renewed. The renewals can be done by special forms obtainable from the clerk to the Licensing Justices or by letter of application. Generally there is no obligation on the licensee to attend the renewal session.

Licences may be transferred from one person to another by consent of the Justices. This is quite common, for example, when one manager takes over from another. The Justices will allow a transfer if they are satisfied that the transferee (i.e. the new holder) is a fit and proper person to hold a licence.

LICENSING REFORM

England

Discussions on licensing reform in England and Wales have been going on for years and repeated attempts to introduce changes have had limited success. Opposition to existing legislation on this subject is widespread. Brewers in particular find the law a hindrance to the development of business. The British Tourist Authority have also indicated that the tourist industry would benefit considerably from more relaxation of the Licensing Law. A strong argument for changes points to Scotland's more flexible licensing system. Evidence available indicates that the lifting of restrictions in Scotland in 1976 has not produced the anti-social problems which were anticipated as a result of easing restrictions.

In the Queen's Speech to Parliament following the May 1987 General Election, the Government have indicated a desire to introduce a more flexible licensing system. At the time of writing, this is anticipated to mean a change in permitted hours with possible opening from 11 a.m. to 11 p.m.

On 2 May 1987 the Licensing (Restaurant Meals) Act 1987 became law. This was a step forward for changes in the law. The Act which amends two sections of the Licensing Act 1964 enables restaurants to serve drinks with meals continuously from lunchtime through to evening service. The new regulation removes the 'dry hours' from 3 p.m. to 5.30 p.m. However, the service of drinks must take place for consumption as an ancillary to a table meal. Pubs without restaurant facilities are, therefore, excluded from this relaxation in the law.

Scotland

In 1976 changes in the system of licensing was introduced in Scotland under the Licensing (Scotland) Act 1976. In Scotland licensing is controlled by a Licensing Board who can issue any of the following licences and can impose conditions in individual premises.

(a) **Hotel licence** permits consumption on or off the premises.
Restricted hotel licence permits residents and guests entertained by them to drink alcohol. It is also applicable to non-residents provided they are taking table meals on the premises. The premises must be structurally suitable to provide a main midday or evening meal or both. The premises must not have a bar counter.

(b) **Restaurant licence**. Consumption of alcoholic beverages must be with table meals. The premises must not have a bar counter and must be structurally adapted to serve the customary main midday or evening meals or both.

(c) **Refreshment licence**. The same conditions apply as those of a restaurant licence except that consumption on the premises will be allowed when food and non-alcoholic beverages are also on sale and not necessarily with table meals.

(d) **Public house licence** permits consumption on or off the premises.

(e) **Off-sale licence** is for consumption off the premises only.

(f) **Entertainment licence** permits consumption on premises providing public entertainment, e.g. cinemas, theatres, dance-halls. However, the sale of alcoholic drinks must be ancillary to the entertainment provided.

(g) **Occasional licence**. This authorises a licence holder (but not of refreshment or entertainment licences) to sell alcoholic beverages outside the licensed premises during the course of a catering event. The day and hours must be determined by the Licensing Board which may also impose other conditions. Any breach of the conditions is an offence.

Permitted hours The permitted hours in Scotland are very similar to those in other parts of the mainland. Weekdays 11 a.m. to 2.30 p.m. and 5 p.m. to 11 p.m. and on Sundays 12.30 p.m. to 2.30 p.m. and 6.30 p.m. to 11 p.m.

However, Licensing Boards in Scotland may grant extensions to the permitted hours depending on social customs in their localities. These extensions, which can be of a permanent nature, have introduced great flexibility to opening hours. In effect licensed premises in Scotland can open before 11 a.m. during the afternoon break and after 11 p.m.

The Licensing Boards have power to make Restriction Orders restricting evening permitted hours till 10 p.m. if conditions are such as to create a public nuisance or a threat to public order or safety.

TRADE DESCRIPTIONS ACTS 1968 AND 1972

The Trade Descriptions Act 1968 replaced and expanded the old Merchandise Marks laws dealing with the misdescription of goods. It brought a new dimension into the field of consumer protection by making provisions for the criminal prosecution of breaches.

In 1972 the Act was supplemented by requiring an accurate indication of the origin of certain imported goods. It is an offence under this Act during the course of business to supply or offer to supply goods which have been manufactured or produced abroad without clearly disclosing the country of origin. Statements such as 'British Made' are not sufficient, they must be supplemented with the name of the country from which the goods originate. Both Acts are linked together as the Trade Descriptions Acts 1968 and 1972, and unless stated otherwise all references to the Act in this chapter will refer to the 1968 Act.

Section 1 states that 'Any person (here person includes a limited company) who in the course of a trade or business (i.e. transactions of a commercial nature):

(a) applies a false trade description to any goods; and
(b) supplies or offers to supply any goods to which a false trade description is applied;

shall, subject to the provisions of this Act be guilty of an offence.'

Section 4 elaborates on the word 'applied'. A trade description to goods is applied if any mark is affixed, annexed or incorporated either to the goods or its package in whatever form. An oral statement by the seller may amount to a trade description.

Section 2 defines trade description, and in an endeavour to clarify the definition lists ten subsections covering all areas of description. These are listed below from (a) to (j) with examples of how they may apply to a catering or hotel situation.

(a) Quantity, size or gauge (450 g; a 16 in. baking tin).
(b) Method of manufacture or production (Paté de Maison).
(c) Composition (60% pork; 10% rusk).

(d) Fitness for purpose, strength, performance, behaviour or accuracy (suitable for children).

(e) Any other physical characteristics (free from additivies).

(f) Testing by any person and the results thereof (all chefs asked prefer to use Nord Products).

(g) Approval by any person or conformity with an approved type (approved by the North-West Regional Health Authority).

(h) Place or date of manufacture, production or processing (Chateau Latour, first growth, Pauillac).

(i) Person by whom manufactured, produced or processed (bottled by Pedro Domecq).

(j) Other history, including previous ownership or use (aged for 12 years in our cellars).

Under **Section 12** is covered the false indication of Royal Patronage or approval of a particular food product as well as false indication with regard to the supply of goods to a particular person or organisation, e.g. Meat Suppliers to the National Health Service.

False price indications are dealt with by **Section 11**. The Act covers false comparison with a recommended price and false comparison between a current price and a previous one, also indications that the price is less than it really is. The act does not deal with every kind of untrue statement which might be made about prices, e.g. a trader may say that his price is lower than someone else's and it is up to the customer to verify this claim.

A trade description may also be applied by means of an advertisement, and under **Section 5** an offence is committed if goods are falsely described in advertisements. A catalogue, circular or price-list are forms of advertisement so that poetic licence when writing menus can lead to an offence.

Local weights and measures authorities are under a statutory duty to enforce the provisions of these Acts. The inspectors are empowered to enter, inspect and seize and make test purchases. While they may prosecute in their own names, in practice this is done by a solicitor from the council's Trading Standards Department. It is a separate offence to obstruct one of these inspectors in pursuance of the Act.

WEIGHTS AND MEASURES

A licensee has a duty to sell liquor only in recognised quantities as stipulated under the Weights and Measures Act 1963 and regulations issued under the Act. Retail sale of draught beer and cider may only occur in quantities of $\frac{1}{3}$ pint, $\frac{1}{2}$ pint or multiples of $\frac{1}{2}$ pints. Exception to this rule is for mixed drinks like, for example, shandy. Unless beer is being served from a pump with a pre-set measuring device sealed by HM Customs and Excise, it can only be served in a Government stamped glass of either 25 or 50 centilitres (cl) ($\frac{1}{2}$ pint or 1 pint).

The retail sale of gin, vodka, rum and whisky is only allowed in quantities of $\frac{1}{4}$, $\frac{1}{5}$, or $\frac{1}{6}$ of a gill or in multiples of these. The establishment is free to choose its own measurement provided it is prominently displayed for the customer to see and provided the same measure is sold throughout the premises. An exception is made for the preparation and sale of cocktails.

Under the Weights and Measures (Sale of Wine) Order 1976 wine sold for consumption on the premises, whether or not pre-packed, must be sold only in quantities of 25 cl, 50 cl, 1 litre, 10 fl.oz or 20 fl.oz, unless it is pre-packed in a securely closed bottle or sold by the glass or other vessel. This regulation is of particular importance to the sale of wine by carafe.

Furthermore the licensee must display for the information of customers, or include on every wine list and menu, a notice stating the quantities in which such wine is for sale for consumption on the premises. The Department of Trade have introduced three new legal metric measures namely, 125 ml, 150 ml and 175 ml.

Under the 1963 Act the licensee cannot avoid liability, no matter how much control is exercised, for offences in breach of the Act committed by any member of staff.

When a Trading Standards Officer calls on the premises he will:
1. Check all stamped or sealed measures;
2. Ensure that 1-pint and $\frac{1}{2}$-pint glasses for draught beer bear the Government stamp;
3. Seek for evidence of adulteration or dilution;
4. Check that measures provided are clearly displayed;
5. Check that the price-list shows prices inclusive of VAT.

ASSIGNMENT

1. What is the main purpose of the Food Act 1984?
2. Give the legal definition of 'food'.
3. Explain briefly the labelling regulations.
4. The Food Act 1984 deals with the food hygiene regulations. Explain briefly.
5. State what are the powers of an Environmental Health Officer.

6. What is a Justices' licence?
7. What does the term 'permitted hours' mean?
8. Explain briefly the difference between a residential licence and a restaurant licence.
9. List the categories into which an 'on-licence' fall.
10. Explain briefly the difference between a General Order of Exemption and a Special Order of Exemption.
11. What does 'drinking-up time' mean?
12. In which month is the Annual Licensing Meeting held?
13. Explain briefly the purpose of the 1968 and 1972 Trade Descriptions Acts.
14. Give five examples of how the Act clarifies the definition of trade description.
15. Explain what regulations the Weights and Measures Act 1963 imposes on the retail sale of draught beer.

16

SETTING UP A BUSINESS

Before even contemplating the idea of a business, the person must first take a look at himself/herself and find out whether he has the personal characteristics to be a business person. Running a small catering business cannot be looked at simply as earning a living by exercising one's love of cooking. Running a catering business first of all requires good health and stamina to deal with the long and unsociable hours that catering demands. The courage to take risks without being frightened of the consequences and the perseverance to continue when things go wrong are both essential. While organising skills can be developed, the organising ability must be there. Liking people and being able to socialise easily is important in a catering venture. The support of the family is of the utmost importance to a small business person. The family must fully understand what going into business means. The involvement of the family is unavoidable. There may be a need to cope with a small income initially. There must be a willingness to accept the financial risks involved. Once satisfied of this total commitment to the success of the business, the next step is to consider realistically the kind of business best suited to one's skills and financial capabilities. The dream of owning a small country hotel or pub is shared by many, but without adequate planning and research this dream can all too easily become a nightmare. Only one basic trading idea at a time can be developed properly. When the choice has been made, whether it is a transport café, a home catering service, a restaurant, a hotel or a tea-room, then all efforts must be concentrated on preparing a detailed plan for the development of ideas into a worthwhile business.

There are basically three ways of going into business.
● One is to start from scratch developing one's brainchild.
● The other is to buy an existing business which can be developed further.
● The third alternative is to buy a franchise.

All three share the same pitfalls. They all require thought and study and of course finance. All three possibilities must be included in the initial plans, each one looked at carefully and the choice best suited made.

STARTING FROM SCRATCH

Starting from scratch is possibly the hardest since the venture is an unknown one. All estimates on expenditure can be accurately worked out. Estimates on income are more difficult to calculate because it involves financial as well as market considerations. Looking for suitable premises is time consuming and expensive. There may also be problems with planning permission. Whichever type of establishment has been decided upon, will require a concentration of people with similar needs and tastes. The much-used quote of 'location, location, location' as the three most important factors making for a successful hotel applies to any catering venture today as much as it did then. Even though eating out is increasing as part of leisure pursuits, siting catering establishments has become more difficult because of the economically and socially complex composition of today's consumers. Passing trade is not the sole factor, but is one of a combination where attracting the appropriate type of trade plays an important role.

EXISTING BUSINESS

One of the advantages of buying an existing business is the knowledge available from the history of the establishment. This can enable the new owner to start right away and introduce changes gradually. The first information required is the *real* reason why the owner wants to sell. Common reasons are early retirement, old age, ill health, a more demanding interest in another venture or sometimes boredom with the business. The fact is that very few flourishing businesses are sold and any excuse for the sale must be taken with a pinch of salt. It is therefore important to go through the accounts carefully. Sometimes poor trading results are dismissed as 'shown for tax purposes'! This may or may not be the case. The truth will be difficult to ascertain and therefore the accounts have to be read as they are and not as they ought to be. This is where the services of an accountant comes in useful. The accountant would be able to compile considerable information from audited accounts which ought to go back, preferably, for a minimum period of at least three years. This information would give an indication of the patterns on salary, on expenses and profitability.

A few visits to the area at different times of the day can give some indication of trading patterns and information on what type of customer is seen in the area. The competition can be judged. Sometimes competition is better than no competition at all. If the competition is doing badly it is possible that the area is bad for this type of business. These points will be helpful in assessing the goodwill, that is, the price being asked for the going concern.

A solicitor will be able to obtain information on any plans for the area when the conveyancing searches are made. The use of a solicitor at an early stage can save money later, particularly if there are partners involved. Choosing the right accountant is also very important. Many accountants are only used for the preparation of audited accounts or for dealing with tax enquiries. A good accountant can be very useful in the early stages of going into business.

FRANCHISING

Franchising is increasing in popularity in this country. Spuds-U-Like, Strikes, Kentucky Fried Chicken, Wimpy, Pizza Express are but a few. It allows the franchisee, that is, the operator, to use the trading name of the franchisor, that is, the franchise company. One of the advantages to the operator is that although the operation is run independently the business carries an established reputable name. The franchisee gets training and advice and benefits from national advertising, bulk purchasing and assistance with raising loans. Although the business risk is reduced it must be stressed that success will still depend on the hard work and skills of the operator. The main disadvantage is the payment of the franchise fees. These are twofold: the 'set-up fees' which range from £15,000 to £400,000; and the management fees or royalties which are based on turnover (not profit) and range from 3 to 10 per cent. Another disadvantage is that normally there are certain restrictions on the sale or transfer of a franchise business. Prospective franchisees should seek advice from a bank manager or solicitor before entering into any agreement.

BUYING OR RENTING

The question of buying or renting premises must be considered although of course it must be appreciated that the decision can be governed by the availability of the suitable building meeting the planned requirements. Buying is definitely a better proposition since it means acquiring an asset which appreciates with time and there would be a capital gain (subject to tax) if it were sold at a later stage. Apart from the fact that suitable small freeholds will not be easy to find there will be the problem of finance. Although loans are available for the purchase of premises the operator will have to provide funding which would probably be best as capital for purchasing or to assist with cash-flow requirements. However, a good accountant should be able to advise. Renting is usually a form of leasehold. Unless an old lease is being taken over, leases nowadays tend to be short, about 7 to 10 years with rent reviews in between. A full-repairing lease should be avoided as well as multiple occupancy (e.g. restaurant with occupied flat above). These are matters for discussion during the negotiation stages. The annual rent will depend on whether or not a lump sum premium is being paid, but it should nevertheless reflect current market forces. Any local estate agent will be able to advise. The landlord can interfere with what the tenant can and cannot do unless provisions have been agreed to prevent this. From the outset, whether buying or selling, the use of a solicitor is advisable. Cutting corners with DIY conveyancing can have disastrous consequences.

OWNERSHIP

Having decided on the type of business and the type of premises, the form of ownership must also be decided. The legal entity of the proposed business is important in order to establish the appropriate relationship with the tax authorities, banks and other official bodies.

SOLE TRADER

The simplest form is that of sole trader since there are no formalities other than those connected with business names under the Companies Act 1981. The operator takes full responsibility for running the business and enjoys all the profits, but is also personally liable for all debts and obligations of the business.

Income tax and National Insurance are those of a self-employed person.

PARTNERSHIP

Another form of business is a partnership when there are two or more owners. All partners share the profits of the operation and similarly all partners are liable for the debts of the business. Taking a partner is a very serious step which requires much thought. If at all possible, partnerships ought to be avoided. If a partnership is necessary then it is imperative from the outset to have a properly drawn up agreement by a solicitor. Innumerable friendships and even families have come to grief over business arrangements that have turned sour. In every partnership every partner should contribute something that the other partner could not provide. Thus the partner must offer either money or expertise that the operator could not afford to obtain or hire.

LIMITED COMPANY

The third form of ownership is that of a limited company. The main advantage of a limited company is its legal entity from that of the owner which can also be a disadvantage. It is not difficult to form a company and a solicitor or accountant can easily do that. However, there are annual returns to be made and the operation must be run under a formal structure. For a small business, a limited company is no longer as popular as it used to be. A limited company is probably better at a later stage when profits reach a level where tax advantages require this course. Bank and finance companies will not lend to small companies without personal guarantees, and even landlords increasingly require personal guarantees from the directors before granting leases or agreeing to transfers of leases.

FINANCE AND INSURANCE

Most new businesses require capital which the operator cannot provide solely and therefore turns to someone for an investment of capital. In order to raise finance, the operator must first examine his own personal assets and convert as much of that as possible into capital. Another form is loans from friends and relatives, and here a properly drawn up agreement by a solicitor is necessary to avoid problems in the future. The Business Expansion Scheme was set up by the Government to encourage investors to provide funds to small businesses in return for advantageous tax concessions. There are a number of specialists that keep details of potential investors. There are some Government bodies which might help depending on the type of catering business and on location.

However, the most common or popular place to turn to for money is the local bank. Banks do not lend money freely or easily. The bank manager needs to be convinced. The project must be properly presented and substantiated with facts. Optimism or wishful thinking is not enough. The bank will want to know personal details about the operator, such as his expertise, experience and personal means, and details about the proposed venture. If it is an existing venture the bank will want to study the past accounts and up-to-date liquid figures. This information is best presented in clear concise plans which must also include details of any key personnel. A realistic appreciation of the market will also have to be presented. One important piece of information that the bank will require is a cash-flow forecast. This requires detailed thought on monthly income and expenditure, and perhaps it might be best for an accountant to prepare it. Banks do not part with money easily, and therefore the plans must be carefully prepared and well presented. Banks do not generally lend money without security. Security is the personal guarantee of any loan. This is often referred to as collateral. Security can be in the form of a personal guarantee from someone of financial substance. It can also be in the form of a building or valuable life insurance which, if the business failed, could be sold and the proceeds used to repay the loan. Many small business people use their houses as security. Unfortunately, if the business fails he and his family find themselves homeless. In certain cases if the bank is satisfied that the venture will be successful but the borrower cannot provide any security an approach is made to the Government Loan Guarantee Scheme. This is a scheme set up by the Government to assist small businesses by guaranteeing up to 80 per cent of the loan. It is not a cheap way of raising money as interest is high, but it may be the only way of raising capital.

Many suppliers are willing to risk supplying goods and services on credit, and while this should not be depended upon, nevertheless it is a useful contribution to the working capital of a small business. Another aid is to buy equipment on hire-purchase which means that the repayments can be spread without having to raise a lump sum. Hire-purchase, of course, can also be expensive because interest rates are normally quite high.

Insurance is a necessity a business cannot do without. There are a variety of insurances suitable for different purposes. Employers' liability and public liability are two insurances required by law. The insurance for premises will probably be a condition of the lease. The equipment, furniture and fittings would be an enormous cost to replace and therefore these ought to be insured. The same applies to stock. Depending on how valuable the driving licence is, there is insurance cover in case of suspension by a court. Legal insurance policies are also available to cover against prosecution under any of the many laws and regulations the business is subjected to. There is also insurance available to guard against financial loss caused through fraud and theft by dishonest staff. An insurance broker will be able to advise. It would be wise to remember that insurance is expensive but it is a vital precaution. One fire can easily wipe a business out of existence.

There are over 30 Acts of Parliament and regulations affecting the caterer. Some of these have been outlined in the foregoing chapters, the majority have not even been mentioned. It would be wise to become acquainted with as much of the legislation as possible. Public libraries are useful places for this purpose.

Advertising is expensive and can be wasteful if not thought out well and planned properly. There are of course advertising agents, but for a small business their charges are normally prohibitive. So plenty of thought and ingenuity is required before embarking on an advertising campaign.

Finally, in the foregoing chapters the principles of control have been outlined. These principles are applicable to any organisation regardless of size. The adaptation of these principles must suit the particular organisation, its size and requirements. It is important to appreciate that the vast number of businesses that cease trading do so either because of bad planning or lack of any planning, or because of cash-flow problems created in most cases through lack of proper planning. Planning is an important word to remember in business.

PART IV

Appendix 1

CATERING CALCULATIONS – SELF-ASSESSMENT

The purpose of this test is to help you assess your numerical competence. You must answer all questions then check the answers on page 164.

1. 2,364 + 174 + 285 + 1,464 =

2. 6,472 − 4,598 =

3. 2,462 × 246 =

4. 9,594 ÷ 123 =

5. (62 + 4) − (30 + 11 + 14) =

6. (60 − 20) + (40 + 10) − (20 − 5) =

7. (82 × 5) + (60 + 2) + (3 × 4) − 12 =

8. (20 + 2) × (5 + 7) =

9. Four crates of beer bottles contain 20, 16, 24, 10 bottles. How many beer bottles are there all together?

10. A complete shelf can contain 60 tins of shandy. If there are 17 tins on the shelf how many more tins do you need to fill the shelf?

11. You are to prepare sandwiches for two functions. One of the functions is for 175 people who are allowed two sandwiches each. The other function is for 56 people who are to be provided with three sandwiches each. How many sandwiches do you need to make?

12.   A grateful customer leaves a box of chocolates to be divided among six waitresses. How many chocolates will each waitress get if the box contains 48 chocolates?

13.   At the end of a shift four waiters hand in their takings of £64.20, £41.36, £18.49, £57.68. What is the total amount handed in?

14.   After paying a bill for £37.88 a customer notices he was overcharged by £4.79. How much should the correct bill have been?

15.   How much would a waiter earn for working 7 hours if he is paid £2.27 per hour?

16.   The tronc which has to be shared equally between 13 employees contains £228.41. How much will each employee get?

17.   Add 177.23 + 62.05 + 15.17

18.   Deduct 2,919.87 from 6,476.76

19.   Multiply 2,647.22 by 22.34

20.   Divide 67.21 by 13.23

21.   A recipe requires 8 oz of sugar. How much would that be in grams? (1 oz = 28.35 grams)

22.   A block of margarine weighs 340 g. How much does it weigh in ounces?

23.   What would be the equivalent in pints of 2 litres of watercress soup? (1 litre = 1.76 pints)

24.   Calculate what 3 pints of cream would be in litres?

25.   If your oven is in °C what temperature should you use if the recipe recommends 400 °F?

26.   The cook book says 220 °C and your cooker is in °F. At what temperature should you set your oven?

27. Approximately how many yards are there in 18 metres? (1 yard = 0.9144 metres)

28. During the last 4 days 16, 18, 15 and 17 portions of crème caramel were sold. What was the average number of portions sold per day?

29. At 200 pesetas to the pound (£), how many pesetas would you get if you exchanged £30?

30. A hotel receptionist has US $25. What is the sterling equivalent if the rate of exchange is US $1.72 to the £?

31. Add $7\frac{1}{2}$ per cent service charge to a bill totalling £41.50.

32. There are 18 chefs in a hotel kitchen of which 27.8 per cent are women. How many women chefs are there?

33. A carton containing 36 tins of tomato is found to be 6 short. What percentage of tins are missing?

34. What saving would you make at a cash and carry if you are allowed 5 per cent discount on a purchase of £65.00 worth of groceries?

35. A bottle of wine costs £4.79 *including* VAT of 15 per cent. What was the original price before VAT was added?

36. A bill came to £42.60 *including* 6 per cent service charge. What was the amount of the service charge added?

37. What is 11 per cent of £22.20?

38. Express 40 as a percentage of 60.

39. Out of 155 meat dishes served 55 were pork. What percentage of dishes were pork?

40. Find 12 per cent of £142.00.

Appendix 2

CONVERSIONS

Answers to the questions are given on page 166.

This appendix deals with conversions.

The examples below will give you practice and help you become more proficient. Always write the formula first so that you can remember it more easily.

Unlike our currency where we have a metric system (i.e. pounds and pence) the weights and measures in the UK are a confusing mixture of metric and imperial. It follows that recipes in metric measures will need converting into imperial or vice versa. It is therefore useful to remember the following conversion rates which are the most common in day-to-day cooking.

There are 1,000 grams (g or gm) in 1 kilogram (kg).
The imperial counterpart is pounds and ounces these being:
16 ounces (oz) in the pound (lb).
The conversion rate is 28.35 g to 1 oz.
So, therefore, 200 g would equal 7.05 oz (call it 7 oz).

EXAMPLE

We worked it like this:
1 oz = 28.35 g
$$200 \text{ g} = \frac{200}{28.35} = 7.054 \text{ oz (say 7 oz)}$$

EXAMPLE

Similarly, using the same conversion rate we can say that 9 oz equals 255.15 g (call it 255 g).
We worked it like this:
1 oz = 28.35 g
9 oz = 9 × 28.35 = 255.15 g

1. A recipe requires 13 oz of flour. How much flour would you need in grams?

2.   Convert 789 g of rice into ounces.

Before continuing check that you have done these two correctly.

Check 1.   2.
1 oz   = 28.35 g   28.35 g = 1 oz
∴ 13 oz = 28.35 × 13 = 368.55   ∴ 789 g = $\frac{789}{28.35}$ = 27.83 oz
Answer: 369 g   **Answer**: 28 oz

3.   A recipe for Salade de Haricot Blancs requires 200 g of haricot beans. How much will this be in ounces?
4.   For Salade de Viande you need 250 g of cooked meat. Find this weight in ounces.
5.   To prepare Bisque de Homard you require a lobster no less than 560 g in weight. How many ounces should the minimum weight be?
6.   5 oz of grated Parmesan cheese would be equivalent to how many grams?
7.   Calculate 3 oz of butter in grams.
8.   How much sausage meat would you need in grams for Scotch Eggs if the recipe stated 11 oz?
9.   For Minestrone you need 12 oz mixed vegetables and 4 oz tomatoes. Calculate these in grams.
10. Purée de Legumes for four people requires 300 g of mixed vegetables and 100 g of potatoes. Work these out in ounces.

When dealing with pounds and kilograms there are two ways of calculating. Either bring the pounds or kilograms to ounces or grams and use the 28.35 conversion figure or work with pounds and kilograms using as your conversion 1 kg = 2.2 lb.

A bag of rice weighs 6.35 kg. What is its weight in pounds?

Check Answer:
2.2 lb   = 1 kg
∴ 6.35 kg = 6.35 × 2.2 = 13.97 lb
that is, 13 lb and 0.97 lb, i.e. 97/100 parts of a lb
$\frac{97}{100}$ × 16 = 15 oz
Answer: 13 lb 15 oz

There are 98 lb of potatoes ready for peeling. How much would this be in kilograms?

Check Answer:
2.2 lb   = 1 kg
$\therefore$ 98 lb = $\dfrac{98}{2.2}$ = 44.545 kg
Answer: 44.545 kg or 44 kg 545 g

Try the following examples. Do Questions 1 and 2 first and check your answer before continuing.

11. A joint of sirloin weighs 9 kg. Find its weight in lb and oz?
12. Fat and kidney removed from a hindquarter of beef weighs 19 lb 6 oz. What is its equivalent weight in kg?

Check 1.
2.2 lb   = 1 kg

9 kg   = 9 × 2.2 = 19.8 lb

$\therefore$ 8 lb = $\dfrac{8}{10}$ × 16 = 12 oz

Answer: 19 lb 12 oz

Check 2.
2.2 lb = 1 kg

19 lb   = $\dfrac{19}{2.2}$ = 8.636

8.636 kg or 8 kg 636 g

6 oz = 6 × 28.35 = 170 g
$\therefore$ 8.636 + 0.170 = 8.806

Answer: 8.806 kg or 8 kg 806 g

13. A lamb carcass weighing 11 kg was delivered for butchering. What was its weight in pounds and ounces?
14. After roasting, a leg of pork weighed 4 kg 600 g. Find the equivalent weight in pounds and ounces.
15. A consignment of plaice weighs 27 kg. How much is this in pounds and ounces?
16. If a brill weighs 6 lb 14 oz, what is its weight in kilograms?
17. What is the weight in kilograms of a capon weighing 7 lb 4 oz?
18. A turkey weighs 24 lb. What is its weight in kilograms?
19. A chef ordered 58 kg of tomatoes. How much would this be in pounds and ounces?
20. If 76 lb of courgettes were consumed, what would its weight in kilograms be?

Liquid measures are sometimes complicated because of the use of fluid ounces. However, as with weights, conversion from metric to imperial or vice versa is simplified through the use of conversion rates.

Try to remember this:

20 fluid ounces (fl oz) = 1 pint
8 pints   = 1 gallon

1,000 millilitres (ml) = 1 litre
100 centilitres (cl)   = 1 litre
10 decilitres (dl)   = 1 litre
1 fluid ounce (fl oz) = 28 millilitres
1.76 pints   = 1 litre

For eight portions of Tortue Claire you need about 4 pints of good-strength consommé. How much would this be in litres?

Check Answer
1.76 pints = 1 litre
4 pints   = $\frac{4}{1.76}$ = 2.27 litres
Answer: 2 litres.

A recipe for Crème Saint-Germain uses 500 ml of water. How many fluid ounces is this?

Check Answer
28 ml = 1 fl oz
500 ml = $\frac{500}{28}$ = 17.85 fl oz
Answer: 18 fl oz

Remember always to write the formula when answering the questions. Answer 1 and 2 first and check the answers.
21. For mutton broth use 2 pints of water. What is this in litres?
22. Vichyssoise uses about 200 ml of cream. Express this in fl oz.

Check 1.
1.76 pints = 1 litre
2 pints   = $\frac{2}{1.76}$ = 1.14 litres (say 1 litre)
Answer: 1 litre

Check 2.
1 fl oz = 28 ml
200 ml = $\frac{200}{28}$ = 7.14
Answer: 7 fl oz.

23. If you use 5 fl oz of cream to make Crème de Carrottes. What is this in millilitres?
24. A recipe of Crème Reine states 10 fl oz of cream. Calculate

this in millilitres.

25. For Kari d'Agneau a recipe states 1.5 litres of water. Convert this to pints.
26. How much brown stock would you use in fluid ounces for Haricot Mutton if the recipe states 750 ml?
27. To make brine you need 1 gallon of cold water. How many litres is this?
28. When making vanilla ice-cream you use 375 ml of milk. Convert this to fluid ounces.
29. Convert 100 ml of water to fluid ounces.
30. If you are using 5 fl oz of milk for an Ambroise pudding what would its equivalent be in millilitres?

TEMPERATURE

Most of our daily measurements of temperature are made in degrees **Celsius**, (sometimes referred to as Centigrade). The Fahrenheit scale is, however, still in use and therefore conversions are necessary.

To convert from one scale to another a formula is available. So to convert from degrees Celsius (°C) to degrees Fahrenheit (°F) the formula is:

Multiply by 9 and **divide** by 5 then **add** 32 ($\times 9 \div 5 + 32$)

Example to change 30 °C to Fahrenheit:

$$\frac{30}{5} \times 9 = 54 + 32 = 86\ °F$$

To convert from degrees Fahrenheit to degrees Celcius the formula is:

Deduct 32 then **multiply** by 5 and **divide** by 9 ($- 32 \times 5 \div 9$)

Example to change 120 °F to Celsius:

$$120 - 32 = 88$$

$$\frac{88}{9} \times 5\quad = 48.8\ °C$$

The exercises below are for practice in converting from one scale to another. All the statements are factual so you may know the equivalent, but even if you know the answer still work it out by using the formulae. You are given a temperature and you must fill in its opposite scale.

31. Bacteria multiply rapidly at body temperature which is ___ °C or 98.6 °F.

32. The majority of bacteria will multiply at about 15 °C or ___ °F.

33. Milk is pasteurised for 30 minutes at 62.8 °C or ___ °F to make it safe from harmful bacteria.

34. If chilled below ___ °C or 38.3 °F the inside flesh of an apple turns brown.

35. The average temperature for cold rooms is from 1 to 4 °C or ___ to ___ °F.

36. Perishables store well up to a maximum temperature of ___ °C or 50 °F.

37. The rinse-sprays of dishwashers are controlled at around 49 to 60 °C or ___ to ___ °F.

38. Spray taps for washing hands discharge water at a temperature of 48.9 °C or ___ °F.

39. To ensure hand-washed articles are disinfected they should be rinsed with hot water at a temperature of between ___ and ___ °C or 170 and 180 °F.

40. Meat should hang at about 2 to 4 °C or ___ to ___ °F.

41. Chilled meat should be stored at ___ °C or 28.4 °F.

42. The boiling-point of water is 100 °C or ___ °F.

43. The freezing-point of water is ___ °C or 32 °F.

44. The minimum legal temperature for working conditions is 6 °C or ___ °F.

45. Frozen foods are stored at ___ °C or 0 °F.

46. Fresh fish is refrigerated at 6 °C or ___ °F.

47. Most fruits and vegetables are refrigerated at around ___ °C or 43 °F.

48. Dairy produce refrigerates at about 5 to 7 °C or ___ to ___ °F.

49. Melons ripen at over 10 °C or ___ °F.

50. Red wines can be stored at ___ °C or 55 °F.

51. Kegs of beer should be stored at 15 °C or ___ °F.

52. Government regulations forbid chilled butter to be transported at more than ___ °C or 42.8 °F.

Complete the following oven temperature chart by filling in the empty spaces, e.g. the first one should be 248 °F.

	Gas regulo number	Electric Celsius (°C)	Electric Fahrenheit (°F)
Very cool	$\frac{1}{2}$	120	
Cool	1		275
Warm	2	150	
Moderate	3		320
Moderate	4	180	
Moderately hot	5	190	
Quite hot	6		400
Hot	7	220	
Hot	8		446
Very hot	9		473

Appendix 3

PERCENTAGES

Answers to the questions are given on page 166.

Percentages are constantly used in our day-to-day lives. In the High Street we see shops advertising 20 per cent off or we see building societies offering 9.95 per cent on your investment. In business there are many ways in which percentages are used. Percentages are also quite useful as indicators. Rather than saying employment has increased from 3,689,464 to 3,762,528 we can avoid this mouthful by saying that unemployment has increased by 2 per cent. Percentage derives from the Latin word *centum* which means 100. So that 20 out of 100 means 20 per cent. The sign % is short for per cent, therefore 20 per cent is written 20%.

20% is 20 out of 100
85% is 85 out of 100
65% is 65 out of 100

Percentages have many uses in business and in the following sections we shall meet some of these uses. The three most commonly used types are as follows:

1. Calculating percentages of given quantities;
2. Calculating one quantity as a percentage of another;
3. Finding out an original unknown amount after a percentage has been added to it.

CALCULATING PERCENTAGES OF GIVEN QUANTITIES

This is the commonest use of percentages. Like for example finding:
20% off the recommended retail price; 7.5% wage increase; 14% service charge.

The simple rule is:

$$\frac{\%}{100} \times \frac{\text{Amount}}{1} = \text{Answer}$$

So to find 5% of £30.00

$$\frac{\%}{100} \times \frac{\text{Amount}}{1} = \text{Answer}$$

$$\frac{5}{100} \times \frac{30}{1} \qquad = £1.50$$

Find 4% of 660 kg

$$\frac{\%}{100} \times \frac{\text{Amount}}{1} = \text{Answer}$$

$$\frac{4}{100} \times \frac{66}{1} = 26.4 \text{ kg or } 26 \text{ kg } 400 \text{ g}$$

Find 20% of 1,000 guests

$$\frac{\%}{100} \times \frac{\text{Amount}}{1} = \text{Answer}$$

$$\frac{20}{100} \times \frac{1,000}{1} = 200 \text{ guests}$$

Work out the following examples but check your answers before continuing.

1. Out of the 400 diners 20% were French. How many diners were French?

2. A kitchen employs 40 cooks out of which 5% are female. How many female cooks are there?

Check 1.

$$\frac{\%}{100} \times \frac{\text{Amount}}{1}$$

$$\frac{20}{100} \times \frac{400}{1}$$

Answer: 80 diners were French

Check 2.

$$\frac{\%}{100} \times \frac{\text{Amount}}{1}$$

$$\frac{5}{100} \times \frac{40}{1}$$

Answer: 2 cooks are female

3. How much service charge would you add to a bill for £350 if the service charge is 12%?

4. What saving would you make if you were allowed 10% discount on a chef's outfit costing £32.00?

5. 40% out of 36 beer bottles on a shelf are Heineken. How many Heineken are there on the shelf?

6. 35% of a carton containing 360 tomatoes are found to be under-ripe. How many tomatoes are under-ripe?

7. A chef who earns £120 per week is given a 7% pay rise. How much is his pay rise?

8. A hotel employing 130 people decides to reduce its labour force by 30%. By how many people is the staff reduced?

9. An army kitchen discovers that 85% of its 2,038 soldiers prefer cornflakes to porridge. How many soldiers prefer cornflakes?

10. In a school with 620 children 70% eat fish fingers on Fridays. How many children eat fish fingers?

EXTRA PRACTICE

Work out as many of the following as possible.

11. Find 1% of £600.
12. Find 3% of £42.50.
13. Find 17% of 90 litres.
14. Find 25% of 80 lb potatoes.
15. Find 60% of 300 eggs.
16. Find 66% of 840 children.
17. Find 2% of £30,000.
18. Find 9% of £16.40.
19. Find 35% of £27.80.
20. Find 49% of 6,600 students.
21. Find 11% of 77 London colleges.
22. Find 2.5% of 160 small hotels.
23. Find 72% of £980.00.
24. Find 67% of 201 cooks.
25. Find 55% of 600 metres.
26. Find 16% of 78 steaks.
27. Find 7% of £4.50.
28. Find 33% of US $770.
29. Find 10% of 770 soldiers.
30. Find 5% of 690 oranges.
31. Find 47% of £48.00.
32. Find 21% of 320 kg.
33. Find 51% of 110 litres.
34. Find 6% of 400,000 pesetas.

The next most popular use of percentages is in calculating one quantity as a percentage of another.

The simple rule here is to place the quantity being expressed over the quantity being expressed against, then multiply by 100

$$\frac{\text{Quantity being expressed}}{\text{Quantity expressed against}} \times \frac{100}{1}$$

Usually this means the smaller amount over the larger amount × 100. For example to express £4.00 as a percentage of £5.00

$$\frac{4}{5} \times \frac{100}{1} = 80\%$$

Once again the quantities can be money, people or pig's trotters, in fact, anything.

Try the following examples, but check 1 and 2 before continuing further.

35. A box containing 60 oranges is found to contain 15 damaged ones. What percentage of oranges were damaged?

36. Out of 50 cooks working at an hotel 20 are Italians. What percentage of cooks are Italians?

Check Answer

(35.) $\dfrac{\text{Quantity being expressed}}{\text{Quantity being expressed against}} \times \dfrac{100}{1} = \dfrac{15}{60} \times \dfrac{100}{1} = 25\%$

(36.) $\dfrac{\text{Quantity being expressed}}{\text{Quantity being expressed against}} \times \dfrac{100}{1} = \dfrac{20}{50} \times \dfrac{100}{1} = 40\%$

37. Of 120 invoices received, 65 were for wine supplies. What percentage of the invoices received were for wine supplies?

38. Out of a class of 20 students, 3 obtained a credit in their cookery examinations. What percentage of students obtained credits?

39. Out of 20 packets of curry powder, 16 were damaged through flooding. What percentage of packets were damaged?

40. Out of a total of 110 diners, 40 chose Sole Colbert. Calculate the percentage of diners choosing the fish.

41. In a consignment consisting of 80 bottles of whisky, 60 were Black Label. What percentage of the consignment was Black Label?

42. Calculate the percentage of children eating hamburgers if 120 out of 400 do so.

43. What percentage of students attended a butchery demonstration if only 4 out of a group of 24 turned up?

44. Out of every 120 joints of meat cooked in a kitchen 64 are sirloin. What is the percentage of sirloin joints used?

You will remember that when you were calculating the service charge percentage of 10% on a bill for £24.00 you calculated it like this:

$$\frac{\%}{100} \times \frac{\textbf{Amount}}{1} = \frac{10}{100} \times 24 = £2.40$$

This will mean that the total the customer has to pay is:

Bill   24.00
Service Charge   2.40
Total   £26.40

Now assuming you were told that the bill for £26.40 **included** 10% service charge how would you find the *original amount* before the service charge was added. The formula is:

$$\frac{\textbf{Amount}}{(100 + \%)} \times \frac{\textbf{100}^*}{1}$$

$$\frac{26.40}{(100 + 10)} \times \frac{100}{1} = \frac{2640}{110} = £24.00$$

Similarly, if you wish to find out the amount of *service charge* that was added then the formula is:

$$\frac{\textbf{Amount}}{(100 + \%)} \times \frac{\%^*}{1} = \frac{26.40}{(100 + 10)} \times \frac{10}{1} = £2.40$$

(* Notice the difference)

Now try this for yourself, then check the answer. A bottle of wine sells for £5.50 inclusive of 15% VAT. Find:
(1) The price of the wine excluding VAT;
(2) The amount of VAT added.
Remember to write out both formulae before working out the answer.

Answer:

(1) $\dfrac{\textbf{Amount}}{(100 + \%)} \times \dfrac{\textbf{100}}{1} + \dfrac{5.50}{(100 + 15)} \times \dfrac{100}{1} = \dfrac{550}{115} = £4.78$

(2) $\dfrac{\textbf{Amount}}{(100 + \%)} \times \dfrac{\%}{1} = \dfrac{5.50}{(100 + 15)} \times \dfrac{15}{1} = \dfrac{82.50}{115} = £0.72$

Work out the following:
45.   The following bills are inclusive of 12.5% service charge. Find out the amount of the original bill before the service charge was added.

(a) £132.60	(f) £27.84
(b) £72.00	(g) £78.70
(c) £19.52	(h) £64.60
(d) £44.70	(i) £6.50
(e) £125.75	(j) £20.04

46. The prices of the following bottles of wine are *inclusive of 15% VAT*. Find out what amount of VAT was added.
   (a) £8.60 (d) £7.25
   (b) £6.80 (e) £5.95
   (c) £6.95

47. The following bills *include 10% service charge*. Calculate the amount of service charge that was added.
   (a) £90.85 (d) £71.00
   (b) £34.70 (e) £84.70
   (c) £52.20

Appendix 4

QUICK CONVERSION RATES

Convert from	To	
Ounces	Grams	Multiply by 28.35
Grams	Ounces	Divide by 28.35
Pints	Litres	Divide by 1.76
Litres	Pints	Multiply by 1.76
Pounds	Kilograms	Divide by 2.2
Kilograms	Pounds	Multiply by 2.2
Yards	Metres	Multiply by 0.9144
Metres	Yards	Divide by 0.9144
Fluid ounces	Millilitres	Multiply by 28
Millilitres	Fluid ounces	Divide by 28
°Celsius	°Fahrenheit	Multiply by 9, divide by 5, add 32
°Fahrenheit	°Celsius	Deduct 32, multiply by 5, divide by 9

ANSWERS

APPENDIX 1

1	4,287	21	226.89 (say 227 g)
2	1,874	22	11.99 g (say 12 g)
3	605,652	23	3.5 pints
4	78	24	1.70 l
5	11	25	204 °C
6	75	26	428 °F
7	472	27	19.68 yd
8	264	28	16.5 (say 16 portions)
9	70	29	Pts 6600
10	43	30	£14.53
11	518	31	£44.61
12	8	32	5 women
13	£181.73	33	16.6%
14	£30.09	34	£3.25
15	£15.89	35	£4.16
16	£17.57	36	£2.41
17	254.45	37	£2.44
18	3,556.89	38	66.6%
19	59,138.89	39	35.5%
20	5.08	40	£17.04

SELF-ASSESSMENT

Nos. 1–20
If you have less than ten correct answers then you ought to seek help. If you attend college see your tutor who will no doubt try to put you in contact with the college's numeracy facilities. If you do not attend college, perhaps a friend or colleague could help you with your numeracy. You could also call at your local college and find out about its courses in basic numeracy.

Nos. 21–30

If you have not got them all correct then turn to Appendix 2. This will explain conversions. It will give you practice so that you can gain confidence and competence.

Nos. 31–40

All these dealt with percentages, and if you got less than five correct then you ought to turn to Appendix 3, this will help you. It is important that you understand percentages as you will need them not only for your course but also at work in day-to-day use. This book will help you understand and use percentages successfully.

ANSWERS

APPENDIX 2

3	7 oz	30	140 ml
4	9 oz	31	37 °C
5	18 oz	32	59 °F
6	142 g	33	145 °F
7	85 g	34	3.5 °C
8	312 g	35	34–39 °F
9	340 g and 113 g	36	10 °C
10	11 oz	37	120–140 °F
13	24 lb 3 oz	38	120 °F
14	10 lb 2 oz	39	77–82 °C
15	59 lb 6 oz	40	36–39 °F
16	13.597 kg or 13 kg 597 g	41	−2 °C
17	15.113 kg or 15 k 113 g	42	212 °F
18	52.8 kg or 52 k 800 g	43	0 °C
19	127 lb 9 oz	44	43 °F
20	167.2 kg or 167 kg 200 g	45	32 °F
23	140 ml	46	43 °F
24	280 ml	47	43 °F
25	2.6 pints or 52 fl oz	48	41–45 °F
26	26.8 fl oz	49	50 °F
27	4.5 litres	50	13 °C
28	13 fl oz	51	59 °F
29	3.5 fl oz	52	6 °C

Oven temperature chart

248 °F
135 °C
302 °F
160 °C
356 °F
374 °F
204 °C
428 °F
230 °C
245 °C.

ANSWERS

APPENDIX 3

3	£42	29	77
4	£3.20	30	34
5	14	31	£22.56
6	126	32	67 k 200 g
7	£8.40	33	56 l
8	39	34	Pts 24,000
9	1,732	37	54%
10	434	38	15%
11	£6	39	80%
12	£1.28	40	36%
13	15 l	41	75%
14	20 lb	42	30%
15	180	43	16%
16	554	44	53%

17	£600
18	£1.48
19	£9.73
20	3,234
21	8
22	4
23	£705.60
24	134
25	330
26	12
27	32 p
28	$254

45   (a) £117.86   (f) £24.75
      (b) £64.00   (g) £69.95
      (c) £17.35   (h) £57.42
      (d) £39.73   (i) £5.78
      (e) £111.78   (j) £17.81

46   (a) £1.12   (d) 95 p
      (b) 89   (e) 78 p
      (c) 91 p

47   (a) £8.25   (d) £6.45
      (b) £3.15   (e) £7.70
      (c) £4.75

Index